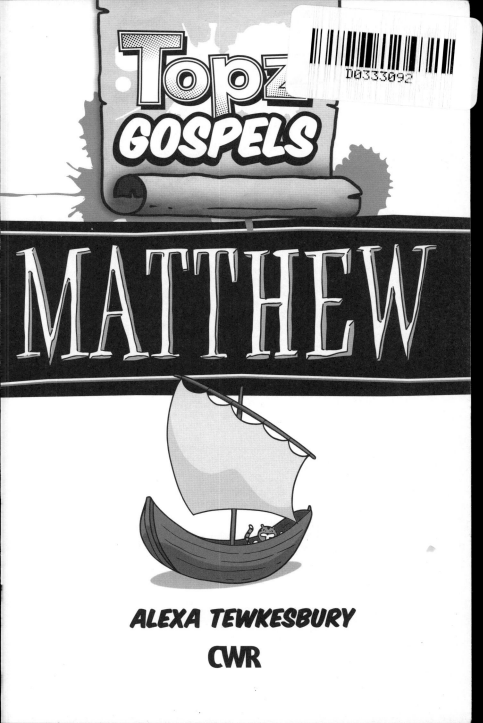

Topz GOSPELS

MATTHEW

ALEXA TEWKESBURY

CWR

Copyright © CWR 2014

Published 2014 by CWR, Waverley Abbey House, Waverley Lane, Farnham, Surrey GU9 8EP, UK. Registered Charity No. 294387. Registered Limited Company No. 1990308.

The right of Alexa Tewkesbury to be identified as the author of this work has been asserted by her in accordance with the Copyright, Designs and Patents Act 1988, sections 77 and 78.

All rights reserved. No part of this publication may be reproduced, stored in a retrieval system, or transmitted, in any form or by any means, electronic, mechanical, photocopying, recording or otherwise, without the prior permission in writing of CWR.

For a list of National Distributors visit www.cwr.org.uk/distributors

All Scripture references are from the Good News Bible (Anglicised), copyright © American Bible Society 1966, 1971, 1976, 1992, 1994, 2004.

Concept development, editing, design and production by CWR
Cover Illustrations: Mike Henson at CWR
Internal Illustrations: Ben Knight at CWR
Printed in the UK by Page Bros
ISBN: 978-1-78259-354-6

Introduction by Sarah

I like to read about Jesus. I open the pages of my Bible and He's there.

HIS LIFE.
HIS WORDS.
HIS STORY.

Everything He taught all that time ago, He teaches to me now.

Every promise He made is still a promise for me today.

Just now, I'm reading the Gospel of Matthew. Matthew writes about how amazing Jesus is – how He came to live with us here on earth; what He taught us about the way to be close to God forever. And when I say 'us', I mean *everybody*! Every single one of us can be God's friend if we choose to be.

But I can't help wondering … what it would have been like to have actually lived in the time of the Bible.

What must it have been like to be there? Actually *there*? To wake up in the morning and know that you could go out and listen to Jesus? To stand with the crowds of people and hear His voice?

What must it have been like to see Jesus face to face?

This is what I wonder.

And when I close my eyes and imagine I'm there – this is how I see Jesus' story …

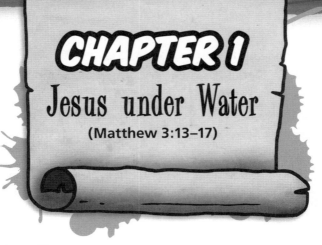

CHAPTER 1
Jesus under Water
(Matthew 3:13–17)

'SARAH!'

John yells at the top of his voice along the dusty path.

Sarah doesn't yell back. Saucy snuggles into her lap. She doesn't want to startle the little cat.

'*What?*' she hisses.

John hurtles up to her. His dog, Gruff, stops a little way off to sniff at a patch of scrubby grass.

'Well, don't just sit there, Sarah!' John cries. 'He's here – we've seen Him! Hurry up!'

'Don't be so loud,' Sarah snaps. 'You'll scare Saucy. What are you talking about anyway? Who's here?'

John raises his eyes. 'Who do you think? It's Jesus!'

Sarah catches her breath. Her twin brother turns and points along the dusty track.

'Topz saw Him walking that way. The others have gone after Him. We'll catch them up if we're quick. But you've got to hurry.'

Sarah scrambles to her feet, Saucy cradled in her arms.

'Tell you what, Saucy,' she murmurs. 'We are *not* going to want to miss this.'

She hurries down the track and calls back over her shoulder, 'Come on, John! What are you waiting for?'

The track leads towards the River Jordan. It's hot, the ground baked hard by the sun, the air still and heavy.

Sarah stops, out of breath. 'John, are you sure this is the right way?'

'Positive.' John nods his head, breathless, too. 'This is the way Jesus walked and the other Topz went after Him.'

'There's no sign of anyone.'

'Just keep going,' says John. 'The river's this way. Maybe they've gone down there.'

They run again.

'There they are!' John points and they run faster.

Up ahead, Topz stand together under a tree. Dave waves and beckons. As the twins get closer he holds a finger to his lips; nods towards the riverbank.

He smiles. 'Look. It's Jesus.'

The Gang gaze at the figure by the water. Jesus is alone.

'Do you think He knows we're here?' Sarah whispers.

Paul shrugs.

They watch as a second man appears on the riverbank and walks towards Jesus. He wears a rough-looking tunic with a leather belt round his waist. This is another John. John the Baptist. He travels around and tells people to get ready for the Lord. To get ready for Jesus, who will teach them about God and how they can be with Him forever.

John the Baptist baptises people in the River Jordan. They come to him from all over. People who want to be friends with God. They say sorry to God and ask Him to

forgive them for the wrong things they do. Then they step into the water with John the Baptist and he gently holds on to them and lowers them down into it – until they're just below the surface. Just for a moment.

When they come up again, they're soaking wet but they look so happy! They know that God has forgiven them. The water has washed away all the wrong things they've done and they have a new, clean life to live.

Jesus and John the Baptist talk.

Topz edge a little closer. Close enough to hear. Sarah still holds on to Saucy. John crouches down. He catches Gruff by the collar to keep him still.

'BAPTISE ME, JOHN,' JESUS SAYS TO THE MAN IN THE ROUGH TUNIC.

John the Baptist's eyes open wide.

'How can I baptise You?' he asks. 'You're Jesus. The Son of God. You're the One who should baptise me.'

Jesus shakes His head. 'No. Baptise me now, John. Please. It's what God wants.'

Topz gaze, open mouthed, as John the Baptist steps into the river with Jesus. They watch him lower Jesus down into the water, then lift Him up again. And that's when something even more astonishing happens.

The most astonishing thing they have ever seen.

It's as if the sky opens high up above Jesus' head. And something like a beautiful dove flutters downwards and comes to rest on Him.

Then a voice speaks out of the sky.

'This is my Son. My very own Son. I am so pleased with Him.'

Topz hardly dare breathe – even Gruff and Saucy stay still.

They watch in silence as Jesus walks away. They lose sight of Him among the trees.

John the Baptist quietly leaves, too.

Once they have gone, there is just the river, which babbles and trickles and flows between its banks.

Danny's voice is soft. Almost a whisper. 'I want to be baptised,' he says. 'I want to know more about what it means. I've never really thought about it before. I just know it's something people do when they want to be God's friend. Really properly His friend.'

Danny looks up. His eyes scan the Gang's faces.

'I want God to know I'm serious about living my life with Him in charge. I want other people to know I'm serious, too … I want to be baptised.'

CHAPTER 2
Followers
(Matthew 4:18–22)

'Race you to the lake!'

Benny yells and runs. He runs fast. Danny, Paul and John race after him, and Gruff pelts along at John's heels.

'CATCH ME IF YOU CAN!'

Benny screeches on. His voice rings out across Galilee's shores. The peace shatters.

Fishermen at the far end of the beach sit beside their boats and mend their nets. They lift their heads and frown: that boy with the floppy fringe makes too much noise. Someone should tell him to pipe down.

Benny is first to the water's edge. He knew he would be. He'd started off with too good a head start.

'Yesss!' he shouts. He throws his arms in the air.

Danny charges up. 'Shhh! They're looking.'

'Who's looking?' Benny asks.

'The fishermen. I think they're cross. You must be scaring the fish.'

Benny turns his head towards them. 'Naah!' he grins. 'They're just gazing in awe at my super-duper speediness. Benny the champion!' he sings out.

Gruff scampers past him into the lake. Just far enough to swim.

'So, Benny,' Paul says, out of breath. 'How long have you been this humble?'

As fast as he is in the water, Gruff bounds out again. He stops on the beach, shakes himself dry and showers Benny in a fine spray.

John laughs. 'Go, Gruff! You know what they say about pride, don't you, Benny?'

'WHAT?' GRUNTS BENNY. 'IT GETS SHAKEN ON BY A SOAKING WET DOG?'

Out on the water, two men are fishing from their boat. They work hard with their nets. Skilful fishermen, they pull them and stretch them and heave them to haul in their catch.

The four boys on the shore stand and watch. They squint into the sunshine.

'Isn't that Simon Peter and Andrew?' says John. He lifts a hand to shade his eyes and peers harder at the two men in the boat. 'It is. I'm sure it's them.'

Paul gazes out at them as they work. 'They're brothers, aren't they?' he says. 'Wonder if today is a good fishing day or a bad fishing day. Imagine having a job like that where you never know. When you get up in the morning, you never really know whether you'll earn enough money or not. Must be hard. 'Cos if you don't earn enough here – what do you do?'

'Hey!'

At the sound of Josie's voice, the boys turn. Sarah and Dave run across the beach after her.

'Look!' gasps Josie. She's out of breath – they all are. **'OVER THERE!** We followed Him from town.'

Further along the shore, Jesus stands by Himself. He watches the two fishermen in the boat on the lake, too. They drag in their nets and begin to sail back to the beach.

Once they reach the shallows, Jesus calls out to them: 'Simon Peter! Andrew!'

They look up from their busyness in the boat. They see the Man on the beach. They know it's Jesus.

He calls to them again. 'Come with me.'

They stare. Is this Man really talking to them?

'Come with me and I will teach you how to catch people for God.'

The two fishermen don't hesitate. They don't stop to ask each other, 'Should we? Shouldn't we?' Instead, they leave their fishing nets, leap out of their boat and run towards Jesus.

Jesus turns and begins to walk away up the beach.

Simon Peter and Andrew follow Him.

Another boat stands on the sand close to the water's edge. Three fishermen, Zebedee and his two sons, James and John, get their nets ready for some fishing on the lake.

'James! John!'

Jesus speaks and the three men turn.

'Come with me,' Jesus smiles. 'Come follow me, James and John.'

No one else says a word. Not even Zebedee.

James and John stop work on the fishing nets, climb out of the boat and join Simon Peter and Andrew. The four of them ask no questions. They simply follow behind Jesus as He walks away from the lake.

'Did you see that?' murmurs Josie. 'They just followed Him. No messing about. No arguments. They followed Jesus – just like that!'

'What did Jesus mean?' John asks. '"I'll teach you to catch people for God," He said. What does that mean?'

Jesus and the four followers are almost out of sight. Dave hasn't taken his eyes off them.

'Jesus will teach them how to be God's friends,' he says. 'Then they can teach the same things to other people. That's how they'll catch people for God. They'll let others know what they need to do so that they can be God's friends, too.'

Benny pushes back his fringe; wipes the back of his hand across his hot, sticky forehead. 'I'm always a bit scared to tell people about God. Well, not scared exactly but … I feel silly. I never really know what to say.'

'Me, too,' sighs Sarah. 'I never even know how to start, so most of the time I don't try. But look at those fishermen, Benny.' Her eyes sparkle. 'Jesus said, "Follow me," and they did. They just *did*! So when Jesus tells us to do something, I think we need to learn to trust Him like that. And just do it.'

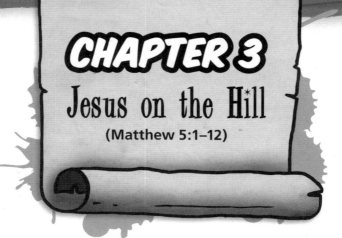

CHAPTER 3

Jesus on the Hill

(Matthew 5:1–12)

A small stone lands neatly in square number four.

Josie hops and jumps along the eight-square hopscotch grid that she and Paul have drawn in the dust on the ground. At square eight she swivels and makes her way back towards the start. She picks up the stone on her return.

'Beat that!' she grins at Paul.

Paul shakes his head. So far he has failed three times to get his stone to land in square number two.

'You're just too good, Josie,' he grunts.

He pushes his glasses up his nose, peers hard at the squares and throws the stone again. It bounces and skips off the edge of the grid.

'Gotta face it,' he sighs. 'I'm just not a natural hopscotcher.'

He glances at Josie. She doesn't look at him. She hasn't even noticed the stone land. Instead, Josie watches the groups of people that have begun to appear and now walk towards them.

'JESUS IS HERE,' she says.

Paul looks around. 'Where?'

'The people, Paul,' replies Josie. 'Look at all the people.'

Paul beams. 'Let's go listen!'

The crowds grow. More and more people join. A sense of excitement builds. Paul and Josie stick close to each other so as not to get separated.

In the distance, Jesus climbs a hill. He wants as many people as possible to be able to see Him and to hear Him. Paul and Josie find a good place to stand and watch.

From His platform, Jesus speaks: 'Listen! I want to tell you about true happiness.'

'Where's the rest of the Gang?' Paul whispers.

Josie shrugs. She doesn't take her eyes from Jesus on the hill. 'Dunno. They'll find us. They'll follow all the people.'

'Those who are happy,' Jesus says, 'are those who know how much they need God. They are the ones who will be with Him forever.

'And those who are happy,' He adds, 'are those who are sad.'

'How can you be happy if you're sad?' Paul whispers to Josie.

She hushes him. 'Shhh! It'll all make sense, Paul. Jesus always makes sense. We just have to listen.'

'When you're sad,' Jesus says, 'God will be beside you to comfort you.'

Josie smiles. 'You see? Perfect sense. If you're sad, you can know what it's like to have God as your comforter. That's one of the times when God can bless you. So, that's something to be really happy about!'

ho are humble,'
, people who aren't
n importance – these
children that God wants

se who want nothing more in
do what God wants them to
are happy because God will give
them i

Josie listei. en mouthed.

'Jesus' teaching, Paul,' she beams, 'it's all back to front! You'd expect to be happy if you do what YOU want, not what God wants, wouldn't you? You'd think living your life your *own* way and doing your *own* thing would be the best thing in the world. But it's not! That's not the way to be happy. God blesses the people who live for **HIM** – who live **HIS** way and not their way!'

There's excitement in the crowd, too. Whispers and murmurs.

'Who is this Man? ... How does He know these things? ... I've never heard teaching like this before!'

Jesus speaks again: 'Happy people are those who can forgive others who may have hurt them or upset them. People who forgive will be forgiven by God.

'And happy people,' He says, 'are those who have pure hearts – who make God happy with the lives that they live. These are the people who will see God.'

Josie feels a tug on her sleeve. Sarah stands behind her. The other Topz boys weave their way through the crowd, too.

'The place is heaving,' says Sarah. 'I nearly didn't spot you at all. Can you hear Jesus from here? Can you hear what He says?'

'Every word,' says Paul.

Josie nods. 'And every word is incredible.'

'Those who are happy are those who want to bring peace,' Jesus says. 'Those who try to stop fighting and arguments; who want to put things right, not make things worse. God will call these people His children.

'And as for those who stand up for God,' Jesus goes on, 'who stand up for God even though other people hate them for it and hurt them for it – how happy are they! They will live with God always. He will keep a special reward for them in heaven.'

Some people in the crowd have begun to sit down, in groups and ones and twos. They listen intently but they look tired. They've walked for miles.

Topz sit down, too.

'What does it mean to have a pure heart?' says Paul. 'Jesus says that people with pure hearts are happy. How do you have a pure heart?'

'Erm ... healthy eating?' suggests Benny. 'Not that I'm very good at that.'

'Not very good?' Danny laughs. 'Bit of an understatement there, Benny. You're rubbish at it!'

Dave grins. 'Anyway healthy eating helps you have a healthy heart, I guess, but I don't think that's what Jesus is on about. A *pure* heart? That's something else. A *pure* heart is about pleasing God. If you live your life in a way that pleases God – if you follow His rules, which are *good* rules because, after all, God knows best because He made us – that helps you to have a pure heart.'

Benny shakes his head. 'But following rules can be hard,' he says. 'I'm not very good at that either.'

'Neither am I,' smiles Josie. 'Nor are any of us. That's normal. And God knows we find it hard. He knows we struggle, so He helps us when we ask Him to.' She looks back towards Jesus on the hill. 'And Jesus says that when we listen to God and do as He says, He can bless us – make us happy deep down inside.'

'So what about seeing God?' Paul asks. 'Jesus says people with pure hearts will "see God".'

Josie looks at him; her head to one side. 'I think that when we live close to God every day, then He lives close to us, too. So we see Him in the good things He gives to us and the good things He does for us. And then one day, when we go to be with Him forever, we'll see Him face to face.'

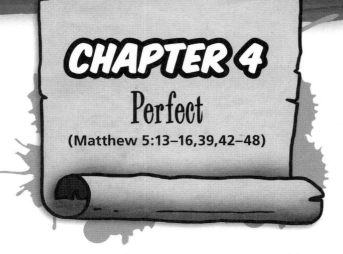

CHAPTER 4

Perfect
(Matthew 5:13–16,39,42–48)

The Topz Gang wait for Jesus to continue speaking. To pass the time, they play leapfrog at the foot of the hill. Other children in the crowd join in.

Soon there are five teams of leapfroggers! They race: each child leapfrogging down the line until the last leaper in each team has finished.

Topz win! They are well practised.

Jesus is still on the hill. For a while, He has sat down to talk with His special friends; His disciples. Now He stands again.

'SHHH!' A hush whispers its way around the crowd. The other leapfrogging children leave their game and run back to their parents. Topz wave to them as they go, then walk further up the hill.

'Do you know what you must be like?' Jesus asks. 'Salt! Salt for all the people on the earth. And you know that if salt stops being salty, it's no good anymore. So it gets thrown away.

'Do you know what else you must be like?' Jesus says. 'Light! Light for the whole world! If a city is built on a hill, you can't hide it. And if you light a lamp at night, the last thing you'd do is stick it away under a bowl. No,' He smiles. 'No, you put it on a lamp stand so that everyone in your house can use its light. This is what you must be like – light that shines so people can see it. If you do good things, other people will notice. Then they will begin to believe in God, and to praise God the way that you do.'

'I understand about being light,' whispers Sarah. 'When a light shines in the darkness you can't ignore it. It's there and it's bright and it's bold. It's beautiful. You wouldn't want to hide it away. You'd want to share it with the people around you who need light, too. If we can shine like lights for Jesus – try to do the things He teaches us, try to obey God – then people *will* notice. They'll see there's something different about us. They'll see there's something different *inside* us. God.'

Danny nods. 'What about the salt?'

'I put salt on my chips,' Benny shrugs, 'but I never thought of following Jesus as like being salty.'

A woman in the crowd behind them laughs.

'I see you don't spend much time in the kitchen,' she says.

'Well, I do,' says Benny. 'But when I'm in there, I'm usually eating.'

The woman smiles. 'Salt is very important to us. Very special. It *is* used to make food taste better, yes,' she says. 'To bring out the flavour. But here we also use it to preserve our food. To make it last longer before we are ready to cook it. Without it, much of what we have to eat would go bad.'

Danny hesitates. He takes in what the woman has told them.

'So if Jesus wants us to be like salt,' he says, 'He must mean we have to make a difference to other people. People who don't know about God. Just like salt makes a difference to the flavour of food.'

'And salt makes a difference in a good way,' adds Sarah. 'So Jesus wants *us* to make a good difference to the people around us – by letting them see how special God is to us. How fantastic it is to be His friend. By living God's way and showing them ... God.'

'But then, how do we "preserve" people?' asks John. 'If salt is used for preserving things, Jesus must want us to be preservers, too.'

Dave looks towards Jesus on the hill.

'I don't think Jesus means us to preserve people exactly,' he says. 'I think He means us to help *save* people from spoiling their lives by ignoring God. To remind them that God is with us; that it's important to live the way He wants us to because that's what's best for us. I think Jesus wants us to keep His teaching alive by *obeying* it – by being it and by living it.'

Once more the woman in the crowd smiles. 'You may

not know about salt,' she says, 'but I think you understand Jesus very well.'

'I don't want to lose my saltiness,' says Dave. 'Jesus says that if that happens, you can't be made salty again. The salt's no good.'

Josie nods. 'God can only use us to tell other people about Him if we're full of Him,' she replies. 'And we can only be full of Him if we stay close to Him. I don't want to lose my saltiness either. Not ever.'

'Listen to me, again!' cries Jesus. 'I am here to tell you how God wants you to live your lives. If someone hurts you, don't waste your time planning how to get your own back. If someone wants to borrow something that belongs to you, then lend it to them.

'And listen to this, too. You are to love the people you don't get on with. More than that, if there are people you think of as your enemies – you are to love them, too! If someone is unkind to you, then pray for them. That's what God wants you to do – pray for them! Then you will be more like Him. God doesn't look at people who ignore Him or do wrong things and say, "Right, no sunshine or rain for you to help your crops grow!" No! God sends the sun and the rain to His friends as well as to those who don't want to know Him.

'Don't you see?' Jesus continues. 'Why should God bless you if you only love the people who love you back? Even tax collectors do that, don't they? And you're not doing anything special if the only people you bother to talk to are your friends. Listen to what God asks you to do, and do it! Your Father God is perfect. Be perfect, too!'

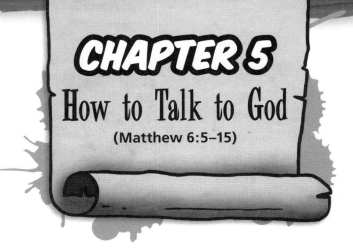

CHAPTER 5
How to Talk to God
(Matthew 6:5–15)

At the edge of the crowd, John throws a stick. It spins through the air away from the people. Gruff pelts after it. Moments later, he's back; tail wagging, stick in mouth.

'Drop it, then, boy,' says John. He puts out his hand and tries to grab the length of wood. Gruff turns his head away. John goes to snatch it, but Gruff shuffles backwards out of reach.

'Come on, Gruff,' laughs John. 'I can't throw it for you if you won't give it back.'

Saucy watches lazily from Sarah's arms. She stretches her front legs, licks a paw, snuggles back down to sleep.

'Seriously, Gruff.' John tries once more. 'Just give me the stick.'

In response, Gruff lies in the dust. He anchors the stick between his front paws and starts to chew it to pieces.

'Great to see you can still rely on Gruff to never do as he's told,' Danny grins.

John raises his eyes. 'Yeah, *really* great. Gruff, sometimes you're just embarrassing.'

From His spot on the hill, Jesus speaks again to the crowd.

'I want to teach you about prayer,' He says. 'When you talk to God, don't show off about it. Don't pray out loud in churches or on street corners just so that other people will look at you and think what a good person you are. Instead, go to your room and close the door. Speak to God quietly. Privately. Other people may not be able to see you, but God will see. God will hear. And He will reward you because He will know that you are serious about your prayers to Him.

'And when you talk to God, you don't need to use fancy words. You don't need to go on and on, as though the only prayers God will listen to are long and complicated. Listen to me! Your Father in heaven already knows what you need – even before you ask Him.'

Paul leans in towards Dave.

'If God already knows what we need,' he whispers, 'then why do we bother to ask Him for anything?'

'God knows us inside out, Paul,' Dave says. 'He knows what we need – probably better than we do. But if we don't spend time praying, how will we ever get to know *Him*? That's how you make friends and keep friends, isn't it? You spend time with them. You talk to them. And anyway, talking to God isn't all about asking for things.'

Jesus' voice rings out from the hill: 'Let me teach you how to pray.'

Dave chuckles. 'You see?' he says. 'God knows we need to learn about this.'

'Our Father in heaven,' Jesus begins.

'May Your holy name be honoured;
may Your Kingdom come;
may Your will be done on earth as it is in heaven.
Give us today the food we need.
Forgive us the wrongs we have done,
as we forgive the wrongs that others have done to us.
Do not bring us to hard testing,
but keep us safe from the Evil One.'
(The Lord's prayer can be found in Matthew 6:9–13)

Josie's face glows.

'We can call God our **"FATHER"!**' she cries. 'God, who made the whole universe wants us to call Him **"FATHER"!** That means we really are His children, aren't we?'

Sarah smiles and nods. 'But we have to honour God's name, too. Be respectful when we talk to Him and talk about Him.'

'And like I say, saying prayers to God isn't just about asking for what we want,' says Dave. 'God wants us to give our lives to Him: "may Your Kingdom come; may Your will be done on earth as it is in heaven." If we ask Him to be in charge of us and we live the way He wants us to, then earth will be more like heaven. Because heaven is God's special home. It's where He really is in charge. Where things are good. Really good.'

Benny stands up. He kicks his legs out to stretch them. 'I know talking to God isn't just about asking for things,' he says. 'But I'm glad we're supposed to ask for food.'

'Not just food,' says John. 'The food we *need*. And the food we need for *today*. It's like God doesn't want us to worry about the future. He just wants us to think about the day we're living in.'

'So it's all about trusting Him,' Sarah says.

'Yeah,' nods Dave. 'But we need to ask God to forgive us for when we do things wrong, too. And we have to forgive other people, but God can help us to do that. He knows we're not very good at getting things right all the time. So when we ask Him to help us to live the way He wants us to – then that's just what He'll do. He'll make us strong. Like Jesus' prayer asks, He will "keep us safe".'

'Cool,' says Paul. 'Good to know.'

'"*Good*" doesn't cover it,' Benny replies. 'It's *stonking*, that's what it is!'

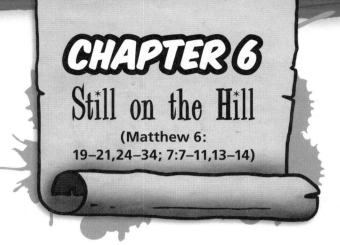

CHAPTER 6
Still on the Hill
(Matthew 6: 19–21,24–34; 7:7–11,13–14)

Gruff lies at John's feet among tattered pieces of chewed stick. He rests his chin on his front paws.

'I like your dog,' says a boy. One of the leapfroggers.

John grins. 'He's called Gruff.'

At the sound of his name, Gruff lifts his head and wags his tail.

'You can stroke him, if you like,' says John. 'He's very friendly.'

The boy crouches down. He puts out a hand and ruffles the top of Gruff's head. Saucy watches from Sarah's arms through half-closed eyes. After a moment, she sits up and leaps to the ground. If there's a chance for fuss, she doesn't want to miss it.

The boy laughs. 'You have a cat, too!'

'Well, Saucy's mine,' says Sarah.

'We have a donkey,' replies the boy. 'She's quite soppy, but she's really stubborn, too. She'll only do something if my dad asks her to. She just ignores my mum and me. And it's only my dad who can ride on her, but that's all right. My mum and I, we like to walk.'

'Have you heard Jesus teach before?' asks John.

The boy shakes his head. 'First time. Not the last, though. I've never heard anyone talk like this. No one teaches like Jesus does.'

Sarah smiles. 'That's because there's no one like Jesus.'

Jesus begins to speak again.

'Think about this: don't spend your time storing up possessions for yourselves here on earth. Why would you do that? Things wear out and get broken, and burglars can break in and steal them. Build up stores of treasure in heaven instead, where nothing can touch them. Wherever you keep your treasure, that's where your heart will be.'

The boy stops fussing Gruff and Saucy a moment. He looks up.

'How can you store up treasure in heaven?' he asks. 'We live here on the earth.'

John still watches Jesus. 'If we love God and ask Him to be in charge of our lives, that's the start of our treasure store in heaven,' he says. 'And when we live our lives for God, everything we do that makes Him happy all adds to that treasure.'

'That's why having treasure in heaven is more important than having treasure on earth, I suppose,' says Sarah. 'Treasure on earth doesn't change your life. Not really. Not forever. And anyway, however much stuff you have, you always seem to end up wanting more. You're never really satisfied. But treasure in heaven? That changes everything. That means that one day you can be with God forever.'

Jesus continues, 'And don't make money the most important thing in your lives. Make God the most important instead. You cannot serve two masters. It just doesn't work to love money and God.

'Besides, you can trust God to take care of you! You don't need to worry about what you will eat and drink, or about what you will wear. Look at all the birds. See how God feeds them! You are worth so much more to Him than they are, so you can be sure that He'll feed you, too.

'And look at the flowers,' Jesus adds, 'if God dresses them to look so beautiful, don't you think that He will make sure you have clothes to wear, too?'

Jesus gazes out across the crowds of people; the upturned faces, some excited, beaming with happiness, some tired and anxious.

'Stop worrying about everything. Your Father God knows what you need,' He says. 'Listen to my teaching. Obey God and live every day with Him right beside you and He will take care of you. He will take *complete* care of you.'

Topz do listen, their eyes bright and eager.

'This is how good God is,' says Jesus. 'Ask Him for something and you will receive good things from Him.

'Seek Him – spend time with Him, listen to Him and do as He asks you to do – and you will find Him. He will stay close beside you.

'Knock on His door and He will always open it. Whatever you need to talk to Him about, whatever you need Him to help you with – God will always have time. His door will always be open to you.'

Jesus pauses and stares far out into the crowd.

'Now think about this, all of you who are dads,' He continues. 'If one of your children asked you for bread because they were hungry, you wouldn't give them a stone instead, would you? No, you'd give them some bread. And if one of your children asked you for a fish, would you give them a snake? Of course not! You would give them a fish. You are not perfect the way God is, but you still know how to give your children good things.'

'But God is a perfect Father! So how much more do you think He will give good things to His children?

'And remember this, too: do for other people what you want them to do for you. Treat others the way you would like to be treated. This is the way God wants you to live your life.'

Gruff gets up. He shakes himself all over. He wanders a few steps away from the boy who fusses his head. He digs and sniffs in the dust. Saucy still sprawls beside him.

The boy straightens up.

'There's so much to think about,' he says. 'If you want God to be in charge of your life, there's heaps to remember. And heaps to get right.'

'But we're never on our own,' smiles John. 'Just like Jesus says, God is always right beside us to help us.'

'We can help each other, too,' adds Sarah. 'All God's friends can help each other. We can remind each other about things that Jesus has taught us.'

'And when God answers our prayers,' Josie says, 'we can tell each other about it. That way we can boost each other up. Encourage each other to keep going. To keep on living the way God wants us to live.'

Jesus says to the crowd: 'If you want to be with God, go in by the narrow gate.

'Take care – there is a much wider gate, too. A wider gate that lots of people slip through because they think the way looks easier. But it's a mistake! The wide gate will lead them far away from God and they will have to live without Him.

'So go through the narrow gate. The way may be hard sometimes, but it will be worth it. Because this is the way that leads to God.'

The boy frowns. 'Where are these gates?' he asks. 'I've never seen them.'

Dave shakes his head. 'Jesus doesn't mean real gates. The gates are like a picture for us. The wide gate stands for living life without God at the centre – for not doing what God wants, ignoring Him, not obeying His rules. And the narrow gate stands for sharing our lives with God and doing as He says. It might not always be easy, but it's what's best for us and it makes God happy. And when we give our lives to Him like that, He promises that we will be able to live with Him forever.'

The boy smiles. 'I'll look out for you. All of you. When I know Jesus is teaching somewhere, I'll look for you. And wide gate, narrow gate,' he adds. 'I won't forget.'

He turns and threads his way through the crowd to find his parents.

CHAPTER 7
The House Story
(Matthew 8:24–27)

Topz lie on their backs at the foot of Jesus' hill and gaze up into the sky.

'Let's play "I spy in the sky",' says Benny.

'What – just in the sky?' asks Paul. 'I don't think that'll work.'

'WHY NOT?' asks Benny.

'Because we've been lying down and looking up at the sky for at least five minutes, and so far I haven't "spied" anything at all.'

'THAT DOESN'T MEAN YOU WON'T, THOUGH' says Benny.

'I've got a better idea,' says Josie. She sits up. 'Let's play another game of hopscotch.'

Paul makes a face. 'I think I'd rather play "I spy in the sky".'

Benny points. 'There's a bird,' he says.

'Where?' asks Paul. He swivels his head from side to side; squints up into the blue arc of sky stretched above them, clear and hot and empty.

'Where?' Paul asks again. 'I can't see any bird.'

Benny shrugs. His shoulders ruffle the dust on the ground where he lies.

'It's gone now,' he replies. 'You have to be quick.'

'So the next time you see a bird,' says Paul, 'are you going to say, "I spy in the sky with my little eye, something beginning with 'b'"? Because if you do, there's no point. We'll all know it's a bird.'

Benny rolls his head towards his friend.

'But it won't necessarily be a bird, will it?' he says. 'It might be a bat … or a butterfly … or a bee … or … a ball.'

'A ball?' Paul raises his eyebrows. 'I haven't spotted anyone playing with a ball.'

'Yes, but, Paul,' replies Benny, 'you didn't spot the bird either.'

From the hill, Jesus calls to His crowd of listeners.

'I have a story to tell you,' He says.

Topz forget their game. They twist over. They scramble to their feet, and brush and pat the dust from their clothes.

'This story is about two men who each build a house,' Jesus begins. 'When someone comes to listen to me teach, and obeys my words, that person is like a wise man who decides to build his house on rock. The rock is solid. It doesn't change or move or crumble – which is just as well. When the rain comes, it pours down so hard and for so long that the rivers burst their banks. And then the wind blows. It roars and howls around the rain.

'But no matter how deep the floods and how strong the winds, that house doesn't fall, because it's built on good, firm rock.

'And what about the other man?' Jesus continues. 'This story is about two house-builders, remember.

'The other man in my story is very foolish. He decides to build his house on sand. Soft, sinking, shifting sand. When the rain comes, once again it pours down and the rivers stream out over their banks. And when the wind blows, it hurls itself about in huge gusts.

'Well, the house on the sand has no chance at all. Down it falls. And what an enormous crash it makes!

'Someone who comes to listen to my teaching, but ignores it and doesn't obey my words – that person is like the foolish man who thought he could build a strong house on sand.'

When Jesus finishes speaking, once more the crowd is full of murmurs.

'This Man is amazing' ... 'I've never heard anyone talk like this before' ... 'Incredible' ... 'Who is He, really?' ... 'He speaks with authority – real authority' ... 'Not like the teachers in church ...'

Jesus comes down from the hill. As He begins to walk away, His shadow ripples with Him across the stony ground.

35

The people follow. In large groups and small clusters and ones and twos, the people follow Jesus.

'I'll be back in a bit,' says Danny.

'Where are you going?' asks Josie.

'Nowhere,' he says. 'Just have to do something. Back in a bit.'

It's still hot but Danny runs. He runs until he's left the crowds behind, until he can find somewhere to be on his own. He runs to the lake.

On the beach, he sinks down and stares out at the water.

Alone on the beach, he talks to God.

Father God, You are so huge and so wonderful and so mighty. I want You to be in charge of my life every day.

And, Father God, I want to hear Jesus' teaching. Every single word of it. But not just hear it. I want to obey it, too. To do the things You ask me to do and live the way You want me to live. I want to help earth be like heaven!

Show me how my life can be like the wise man's house in Jesus' story – built on solid rock. Built on You. Then I'll know that whatever happens and whatever trouble may come along, You'll always be with me. And I'll always be with You.

Please help me not to be like the foolish man. I don't want to ignore You, God. I don't want to build my life without You so that it's like a rickety house on sand. I want to be rock solid. Rock solid for You.

Day after day, Father God. Day after day. Amen.

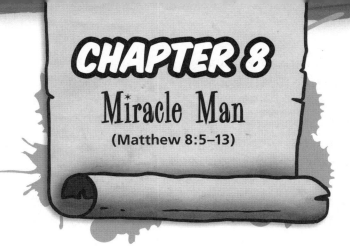

CHAPTER 8
Miracle Man
(Matthew 8:5–13)

Topz wander into Capernaum. The village stands close to the shores of Lake Galilee. They are hungry. Benny has some bread. He shares it out and they munch as they walk.

Somewhere up ahead is Jesus. Somewhere in front of the mass of people who still follow Him.

'Do you think He'll teach again today?' asks Sarah.

'Maybe,' replies Dave. 'As long as there are people around to listen to Him, I reckon Jesus is going to want to teach them.'

'He must get so tired,' says Josie. 'He travels all over the place and people follow Him everywhere. He hardly ever seems to get five minutes to Himself.'

'It wears me out just thinking about it,' grunts Benny through a mouthful of bread.

'And me,' says Sarah. 'Don't get me wrong, I love being around all of you. But sometimes … well, sometimes I like to be on my own, too.'

'And don't get us wrong either,' Benny grins, 'but sometimes we like it when you leave us alone!'

Sarah raises an eyebrow; gives Benny a shove.

'There He is!' Paul points.

Jesus stands in the street. People line the way He has walked and jostle to get closer to Him.

But Jesus doesn't seem to notice them. He concentrates on just one man who stands in front of Him.

'Who's that?' wonders Paul.

Josie shrugs. 'Don't know. Looks like a Roman officer.'

They press forward; straining to hear the conversation.

The officer looks tired and sad. As he talks to Jesus, he hangs his head.

'Sir,' he says, 'I have a servant at home. He is very ill and in bed. He can't move. I know that he is suffering badly.'

Jesus watches the officer a moment. Then, 'I will make him well,' He says. 'I will go to him now.'

The officer glances up at Him. He seems almost timid; afraid to look at Him.

With a shake of his head, 'No, no, Sir,' he answers. 'No, I don't deserve that. I don't expect You to visit my house. But … if You would just order it, then I know that my servant will get better.'

This time the officer looks full into Jesus' face. Into Jesus' eyes.

'You act on God's authority, don't You?' the Roman says. 'You do as He asks You to do, and what You ask for is done.

'In some ways I am like You,' the officer smiles. 'There are officers who are above me and I must do as they say. And there are soldiers who are under me and they must obey me. I order them to go, and they will go.

I order them to come back, and they will come back.
And my servant, who is now so ill … when I ordered
him to do something, he would do it.'

Jesus stares at the man in front of Him; He looks
amazed, as if this is the last thing in the world He
expects the officer to say to Him.

He turns to the people who huddle about Him;
who point and whisper.

'Do you all hear this man?' Jesus says. 'This Roman officer has such huge faith! I haven't found anything like it in the whole of Israel. Let me tell you that people will come from all over the place to hear about God. They will hear and they will learn about Him. Their faith will grow. And one day they will be with Him forever.

'But there will be others,' Jesus adds, 'who will refuse to listen. They will have no faith. They won't want to trust God. And so there will be no place for them.'

Jesus' listeners fall silent. They stare. They watch and they wait.

Jesus looks again at the Roman officer. He smiles at him. Topz can see the kindness, the love in His eyes.

'You can go home now,' Jesus says to the man. 'You believe that I can make your servant well. So your servant is well. It has been done for you.'

The Roman officer bows low in front of Jesus. He backs away. Tears glisten in his eyes.

Then he turns and runs, pushing through groups of astonished onlookers.

'What just happened?' asks Paul. 'Is the servant really well? Has Jesus made him better?'

Josie smiles. 'Of course He has,' she says. 'Because He says so.'

'What's going on? What have I missed?' Danny appears next to them.

'Where have you been?' asks Dave.

'Just to the lake,' Danny replies. 'What's happened?'

Dave's face lights up. 'A miracle, Danny, that's what's happened,' he beams. 'Jesus just worked a miracle.'

CHAPTER 9
The Healer
(Matthew 8:14–17)

Saucy sits under a tree and washes. She licks one front paw over and over, then starts on the other. She pulls down her ears, one at a time. Pulls and smoothes and washes away the Capernaum dust.

Gruff charges at her. He crouches down on his tummy. He runs towards her, stops; chases round in a circle. His tail wags back and forth madly.

Saucy takes no notice. Nothing disturbs her washing routine.

Gruff barks. Barks again. This time Saucy gets lightly to her feet. She stretches, turns her back to Gruff and sits back down. Her wash continues.

'What's all the barking about, Gruff?' John appears. 'You can't be bored already. We've just had a long walk.'

'Looks like he's ready for another one,' says Dave.

'Gruff's *always* ready for another one,' says Sarah. 'He never gets tired. The minute he gets back from one walk he starts to ask for the next.'

In response, Gruff turns his attention to Sarah.

He bounds over to her. He leaps around her and buffets her with his paws.

'John, tell him to stop!' she giggles.

John shrugs. 'No point. He won't take any notice.'

'All right then, Gruff, you win,' sighs Sarah. 'Let's go walking again.'

Instantly Gruff is on the move.

The pair make their way through the village streets. Gruff trots, stops and sniffs, then trots again.

They see Jesus.

He stands with Simon Peter outside Simon Peter's house. The two men go inside together.

Gruff scampers towards the front door.

'Gruff, no!' calls Sarah. 'Come here.'

She runs to catch the little dog, scoops him up in her arms and holds him tight before he can run into the house. She walks a little way further before she stoops to set him on the ground again.

A couple of streets on, a woman hurries past, almost knocking into her.

'I'm sorry,' the woman mumbles. 'I'm so sorry, I didn't see you.'

'That's fine,' says Sarah. 'Are you all right? Is anything wrong?'

'Wrong?' The woman puts a hand to her chest. 'Well, my heart's beating ten to the dozen, but no, there's nothing wrong. It's just …'

'It's just what?' asks Sarah.

'WELL, IT'S JESUS!' the woman cries out. 'You've heard of Jesus? **EVERYONE'S HEARD OF JESUS!'**

Her face shines with excitement. 'Thing is …'

She hesitates.

'Oh, I don't know if I'm supposed to say, but if I don't tell someone, I'll burst, I know I will. It's the mother-in-law of one of our fishermen. Simon Peter's mother-in-law. She's not been well. Not well at all. She's had a terrible fever. Been laid up in bed and everything.

'Anyway, Jesus called in and you'll never believe what happened! He touched her hand. That's all He did – He just touched her hand! And all of a sudden, she wasn't sick anymore. Just like that, she was well again. Just. Like. That.

'And up she got out of bed and started to get a meal ready! I've got to go and tell my daughter. I've got to go and tell her!'

The woman bustles away. Sarah can still hear her chunter to herself as she goes: 'It's a miracle, that's what it is. No more, no less. A miracle as clear as day!'

Sarah and Gruff walk on. They reach the lake. There's a buzz of activity on the shore. It's the end of the day. Fishermen haul their boats up onto the beach. They inspect their catch. They check their nets for any damage and lay them out to dry.

The air cools a little as the sun starts to dip down.

'Come on, Gruff, let's get back,' Sarah calls.

The little dog turns to follow her. He scampers eagerly across the sand and stones, charges ahead of Sarah as she walks back towards the village.

Then Sarah slows.

There's a sound. What is it? Where's it coming from?

She turns her head to listen.

'Gruff!' she calls. 'Gruff, come here!'

Gruff has heard it, too.

A moaning. A sobbing. But not just one voice. Many voices.

Gruff scampers back to Sarah. He paws at her and she picks him up but stays rooted to the spot.

There are people coming. They move slowly. Some hold on to each other and help one another along. Others shuffle through the streets on their own.

Sarah stares. The people move closer. They pass her by as if she's not even there. They cry. Some wail and some groan. These are people full of sickness. People full of pain.

Sarah holds tight to Gruff. She wishes the other Topz were with her. Where are they? Where's Josie? She doesn't want to be by herself watching this; listening to this …

And then Sarah hears another sort of cry. Up ahead at the front of the moaning, groaning people.

This is a cry of hope.

'Jesus! Jesus, please help us! You can heal us. You can make us well. Please make us well!'

The cry begins to spread. It builds and grows and washes across the crowd like a wave – until all Sarah can hear is: 'Jesus! Jesus!'

Her heart starts to thud.

Still clutching Gruff, she keeps to the edge of the crowd. She moves forward with the people. If she can just see what those at the front can see … She stands on tiptoe …

She cranes her neck …

JESUS! HE'S THERE!

And people clamour to reach Him.

Families help sick family members. Friends help ill friends. Those who are alone struggle forward. They all find their way to Jesus' feet.

And Jesus heals them. With just a word.

One moment they are prisoners: prisoners of their sickness. The next they are free.

Sarah watches open mouthed. One after the other they are made well, and there are more tears. But tears of happiness. Miracle after miracle happens right in front of her eyes.

Then she remembers the words she's read in the Bible. This is something Jesus came to earth to do: something to show people how much God loves them. To show them that God has sent Him.

'[Jesus] did this to make what the prophet Isaiah had said come true, "He himself took our sickness and carried away our diseases."' (Matthew 8:17)

CHAPTER 10
Caught Out

'SAUCY!'

Josie calls again. 'Saucy!'

She walks up one narrow street; down the length of another. She peeps into courtyards. She peers up into trees.

'Where are you, little cat?' she murmurs. 'Where have you gone?'

At the far end of an alley, Sarah appears. She gives Josie a wave.

'Still no sign of her?' Sarah says. She's been calling for Saucy at the other end of the village. John, Gruff and Paul are out looking, too.

Josie shakes her head.

'I don't get it,' Sarah frowns. She presses her lips together. She looks as though she might cry. 'Saucy wouldn't just wander off. I know she does at home, but she wouldn't here. She doesn't know this place well enough. She knows she'd get lost. Anything could have happened to her! Oh, where is she, Josie?'

Her friend grabs her hand and gives it a squeeze.

'It'll be all right,' Josie says. 'Saucy'll be fine. We'll find her. She can't have gone far. We will find her.'

Sarah nods. She calls again. 'Saucy! Saucy, where are you?'

'I'll go down to the lake,' Josie says. 'Maybe she's somewhere on the beach.' She twists round, starts to run and shouts back over her shoulder, 'If there's no sign of her there, I'll have a look along the riverbank.'

All the way to the lake, Josie runs. Now and again she slows and calls for Saucy, looks around, and then runs again.

At the edge of the shore, she stops. She leans forward, rests her hands on her knees and gasps for breath.

'Josie!'

She looks up. She can't answer; she hasn't recovered her breath enough. She sees Paul.

'Have you found her yet?' Paul shouts.

Josie manages a grunt. **'NO!'**

Paul points to the far end of the beach. 'I'm going to look over there where the boats are.'

'Hang on a second.' Josie pushes herself upright. 'I'll come with you.' She forces her legs into a jog.

'You look boiling,' says Paul.

'I am boiling,' Josie answers.

They call again. 'Saucy! Saucy!' They make their way carefully between boats pulled up onto the shingle. They step over nets and sails laid out to dry or to be mended. There are no fishermen about. It's late in the day and the last of them have already brought in their catch and headed for home. The smell of fish hangs in the air.

'SAUCY!'

Nothing. No sound. No movement.

'Oh, what are we going to do, Paul?' cries Josie. 'I told Sarah we'd find her. We've just got to find her.'

They call again, picking their way through the mounds of fishing equipment.

Suddenly – 'Shhh!' hisses Paul. 'Did you hear that?'

'What?' Josie replies. 'I didn't hear anything.'

Paul doesn't move. 'Listen.'

And there it is again. Very faint. Almost too faint to be heard.

But they just catch it. It's Saucy!

She meows again.

'Where is she?' says Josie. 'I can hear her, but I can't see her! Where is she?'

They call Saucy's name. They stop and listen. They call again. And at last they find her.

Saucy lies half buried in a pile of nets and tarpaulins rolled up at the back of a fishing boat. Her cries are sad and frightened. Josie and Paul's eyes shine.

'There you are!' laughs Josie. 'We've been looking everywhere.'

'She must have fallen in,' grins Paul. 'Or she climbed in and went to sleep.'

Josie beams all over her face. 'Your Sarah is so worried. Why didn't you come when we called?'

Then they see why.

Saucy is caught up in a net. One back leg is tangled in the mesh and held fast. She pulls and fidgets, but she can't get free.

'Poor thing,' says Paul. 'Come on, let's get you out.'

They pull at the tangle, shake it; try to loosen it.

'If we had some good scissors, we could cut through it,' says Paul.

Josie looks at him. She shakes her head. 'We couldn't do that. Then the fishermen would have a net with a big hole in that needs mending.'

Paul shrugs. 'Well, how are we going to get her out?'

Josie gives the tangle one more tug. The knot doesn't shift.

'I'm getting in the boat,' she says. 'It'll be easier if I can just get closer.' She hops over the side.

Paul frowns. 'Josie, you shouldn't be in there. What if someone comes?'

'Then we'll just have to explain. Come on, help me, Paul.'

Paul sighs and climbs into the boat, too.

Josie kneels on the net pile. Saucy nuzzles her head into the Topz girl's lap as she picks and pulls at the knot. Paul crouches down to fuss the little cat's ears.

Voices carry across the beach towards them. They hear them but take no notice. Until they get louder. And louder.

Paul lifts his head to adjust his glasses. A group of men walk towards them. They look like fishermen. They *are* fishermen! They're friends of Jesus and Jesus is with them!

'Hurry up, Josie,' Paul hisses. 'There are people coming. Jesus is here.'

'I've nearly got it,' says Josie. 'One ... more ... pull ...

'YESSS!'

Saucy is free and Josie scoops her up with delight. 'Let's go.'

'Too late.' Paul crouches low, his eyes fixed on the men who walk towards them.

Josie glances at them, too. 'Might not be,' she mutters. 'Might not be their boat.'

The fishermen with Jesus make straight for them.

'Somehow, I think it is,' Paul mumbles. 'If we get out now, we'll be seen. They'll think we're pinching stuff.'

'But I can explain about Saucy,' says Josie. 'They'll understand ... Of course they'll understand ... Or,' she adds, '... Or we could just hide.'

They hesitate a second.

Only a second.

Then they dive and wriggle down under the nets and tarpaulins; squirming out of sight.

Josie holds tight to Saucy.

'You're going to have to be quiet, Saucy,' she whispers. 'Very, *very* quiet.'

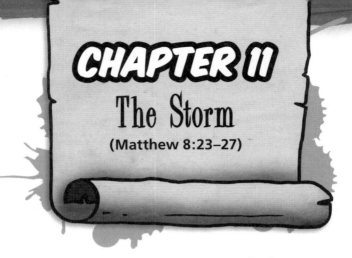

CHAPTER 11
The Storm
(Matthew 8:23–27)

The shores of Lake Galilee seem very still. The sun begins to dip below the horizon and streaks the sky with pink.

There is no one around on the beach. Just Jesus and the friends who are with Him. Perhaps that's why they have come. For a short while, Jesus can escape the crowds that follow after Him. He needs to rest.

When they reach the boat on the shingle, the men haul and push it towards the water. And as the lake starts to lap at the hull, Jesus climbs in. The other men follow. The last one gives a final push away from the shore, then heaves himself up and over the side into the boat.

'All set?' the last man cries. 'Let's sail.'

Paul and Josie hardly dare breathe. They're tucked out of sight; completely hidden beneath the nets and tarpaulins. Their breath wouldn't be heard over the men's talk and the boat's creaks and the splash of the water as the bow cuts through the lake. But they hardly dare breathe anyway.

The men haul on ropes to raise the sail. A light breeze lifts and fills the canvas.

Paul nudges Josie. The tiniest movement. She almost doesn't feel it.

'I'm not good on water,' he says. His voice is less than a whisper. 'Give me a go-kart and I love it. But on water I get seasick.'

In answer, Josie squeezes his arm. She daren't speak. All she can do is cradle Saucy and hope that the little cat stays still and quiet.

How far would they go? Where would they land?

They pick up speed as the sail billows out. The boat rises and falls with the movement of the lake. The men's voices rise and fall, too, as they chat. Sometimes they laugh. Sometimes they fall silent and there is just the sound of water and creaking wood and the cry of seabirds.

But there's a change coming.

Clouds begin to gather in the sky. The pink gashes left by the sun darken and turn deep grey. The breeze blows stronger and the boat begins to rock as waves build and are tossed against the sides. Every now and then, a wave slaps the wooden boards of the hull so hard that it sends a shower of spray over the deck.

The men's voices change with the weather. They're not relaxed anymore. Their tone is anxious. They shout orders to each other. They seem afraid; unsure what to do.

'It's coming in too fast ... Should we turn back? ... Shouldn't we keep going? We're nearer the other shore ... This wind – *IT'S TOO STRONG!* ... *PULL IN THE SAIL! PULL IT IN!*'

Under the nets, Josie and Paul can't see anything.
They can't see the dark clouds or the churning waves.
They can't see the fear that grows in the men's eyes.

But they can sense the alarm in their voices.
They can hear the wind's howl build to an angry roar.
They can feel the boat pitch and sway.

'I FEEL SICK, JOSIE!' moans Paul.

'Me, too,' whimpers Josie. 'We shouldn't have hidden
in here. Why did we hide? We should have got out.
We weren't doing anything wrong. We should have just
told them about Saucy.'

Saucy is scared, too. She clings to Josie; digs her claws
into her arm. It should hurt her, but Josie barely feels
them. She's too frightened.

'I want to go home,' mumbles Paul. 'I wish we could just go home.'

The boat tilts. It goes on tilting.

'We're going over! We're going over!' cries Josie. No one would hear her above the noise of the storm. Even if they did, she doesn't care anymore.

A cry rings out from the deck.

'Where's Jesus? **WHERE'S JESUS?'**

Josie and Paul suck in a breath.

'That's a point,' hisses Josie. 'I'd forgotten about Jesus! I'd forgotten He's on the boat with us!'

'Well, I hope He's a good sailor,' mutters Paul.

'He's asleep!' a voice shouts. 'Jesus is over here and He's asleep.'

'Then wake Him up!' cries another.

The men start yelling out together: 'Jesus! Please, Lord, wake up! **WE'RE CAUGHT IN A STORM.** We're going to sink! Save us! Please save us!'

For a moment, there's nothing more to hear.

Then, through the chaos comes the voice of calm.

'What's the matter? Why are you all so scared? You don't have much faith, do you?' Jesus says.

He stands up. He orders the wind to stop blowing. He commands the waves to settle down.

At once, the storm dies away. The lake lies quiet; hardly a ripple on the surface. The wind drops to a whisper of breeze. The boat rights itself and the sail seems to sigh with relief.

Jesus' friends gaze about. They look at the water's glass-smooth surface. They feel the flutter of cool air brush lightly against their faces.

'How is this possible?' they murmur. 'How? Who is this Man? He commands a storm to stop raging, and it obeys Him!'

Beneath the wave-soaked nets and tarpaulins, Paul and Josie almost laugh aloud.

'He saved us!' mumbles Paul. 'Jesus saved us.'

'We forgot He was here,' says Josie. She hugs Saucy, who shakes her slightly soggy head. 'We forgot Jesus was here with us all the time.'

A frown draws Paul's eyebrows together. 'Jesus is right, isn't He, when He says we don't have much faith.'

'What do you mean?' asks Josie. 'He was talking to the men on the boat with Him. Not to us.'

'But He might as well have been talking to us,' Paul replies. 'Well ... to me. When I remembered He was here, it didn't make me feel any better. I was still scared. I didn't think there'd be anything He could do.'

Josie smiles at him as much as she can under the uncomfortable weight of fishing gear.

'I was scared, too, Paul,' she says. 'And it's all right. Jesus knows we get scared. We just have to ask Him to help us trust Him more. We have to remember He's always there.'

Voices are heard again from on the deck: 'Let's get to shore. Think we've had enough sailing for one night.'

'Great idea,' mutters Paul. 'Think I've had enough sailing forever.'

CHAPTER 12
Believing is Seeing
(Matthew 9:27–31)

'Who would have thought dust could be so useful?' Benny remarks.

With a piece of stick he finishes drawing a three-square by three-square grid in the street dirt.

Dave grins. 'Try telling that to my mum. Dust's got no chance in our house. It's gone before it even lands.'

'I know what you mean,' Benny nods. 'Sometimes I'm sure your mum was born attached to a duster. Mine, too, come to think of it.'

'If you have your own house one day, do you reckon *you'll* ever dust?' Dave asks.

'Nah,' says Benny. 'Don't see the point. I mean, dust's just part of life, isn't it? You know – natural. It's everywhere, so I think it's just meant to be. And if something's meant to be, it doesn't seem right to get rid of it.'

Dave nods. 'Never thought of it like that.'

'So, would you? Dust if you had *your* own house?'

'Nah. Not because dust's meant to be or anything. I just couldn't be bothered.'

Dave crouches down and inspects Benny's grid. 'All set, then?'

'Set and ready,' says Benny. 'Let the Topz noughts and crosses challenge begin. Who's going first?'

'You drew the grid, so you can,' says Dave.

Benny studies the squares a moment. He marks a cross in the centre with the stick; holds the stick out to Dave.

Dave frowns. 'Why do you always do that?'

'Do what?'

'Start off in the middle? With a cross?'

Benny shrugs. 'Why not?'

'Fair enough.' Dave takes the stick. He draws a nought in the square under Benny's cross.

'You see, *I* wouldn't have done that,' says Benny.

'Because?' asks Dave.

'Too obvious.'

'What do you mean, too obvious? There are only nine squares, Benny, and you've drawn in one of them. There are only so many places I can put my noughts.'

'Yeah, but –'

An urgent shout from the far end of the street interrupts him: 'There's Jesus! It's Him, I know it is. I saw Him teaching a few days ago.'

Benny and Dave glance at each other; straighten up. They look in the direction of the voice.

Walking towards them between the small, square houses is Jesus. A few people follow behind Him. Others stand at the edge of the street to watch.

Further back, two men tag along together. Their movements are cautious. Careful. Every so often they pause to listen. As if they're using the noises around them to work out where Jesus is.

'What are they doing?' asks Benny.

Dave watches them. 'Not sure but ... I don't think they can see,' he says. 'I think they're blind.'

The two men walk and stop; walk and stop again.

One of them calls, **'JESUS! JESUS TAKE PITY ON US, PLEASE!'**

Jesus keeps walking.

He is close to Dave and Benny now but before He reaches them, He turns and steps through the doorway of a house.

The group of people who follow behind Him stop outside the door. The two blind men stop, too, for a short moment. Then they push their way through the straggle of onlookers to stand at the doorway. Jesus is inside. They can't see, but they know He's inside. And they step in.

Jesus knows they are there, too.

'DO YOU BELIEVE IN ME?' Jesus asks the two men. 'Do you believe that I can heal your eyes? Heal your blindness?'

The two men don't hesitate. 'Yes!' they cry. 'Oh, yes, Sir, we do!'

All Jesus does is reach out and touch their eyes.

All He says is: 'Let it happen, then. Because you believe it.'

And they can see!

They can see Jesus standing in front of them. They can see each other. They can see the room they're in, just inside the doorway off the street. And they can see the daylight that streams through the opening; the dust that dances in the shafts of sunlight.

They don't speak. They can't. They don't have the right words – not nearly enough words – to say thank You. They can only stand and stare and gasp astonished breath into their bodies.

Jesus has worked another miracle. He keeps working miracles.

'Tell no one about this,' Jesus says. There's a sternness in His tone. A seriousness to His expression. 'I mean it. Tell no one.'

Dave and Benny watch the two men leave the house. The two men who went in blind and have come out with eyes that can see.

And suddenly the two with miracle sight find their voices. They can't keep quiet.

'LOOK WHAT JESUS HAS DONE! SEE WHAT JESUS HAS DONE FOR US!'

They start to run back along the narrow street, calling the news to people as they go. The huddle that has followed Jesus now turns from the doorway and begins to follow the two men.

'Look what Jesus has done! See what Jesus has done!' they echo.

And so the news spreads.

The two Topz boys stare after them. The grid and their game in the dust are forgotten.

'I know Jesus said to keep quiet,' Benny says,

'BUT COULD YOU, DAVE? If you were blind and Jesus made it so you could see – could you really keep quiet?'

'No,' answers Dave. 'No, I don't reckon I could.'

CHAPTER 13

Harvesters

(Matthew 9:35–38)

Danny runs across the bank. He leaps, arms and legs stretched wide, into the river. The splash sprays outwards and soaks the other Gang members. They sit, dangling their feet into the water. They're not impressed.

Saucy scampers for cover behind Sarah.

'Danny!' One annoyed shout from all of them.

'Sorry,' Danny splutters. 'Didn't realise I was so ... heavy.'

Benny's on his feet. 'Bet you're not as heavy as this!'

He runs and jumps into the water next to his friend. The splash he makes is even bigger.

On the bank, Topz groan.

'OI!' shouts Danny.

'What are you moaning about?' Benny laughs. 'You're soaked through anyway.'

'Bet I can beat you to the other side,' says Danny.

'Bet you can't,' Benny answers.

Danny glances towards the bank. 'Start us off someone.'

The Gang still look cross from the splashing.

Paul gets to his feet, unhooks his glasses and wipes away the drops of water. 'At least if you're the other side you can't keep getting us all wet,' he says.

'Yes, we can,' Benny grins. 'Because we'll be back.'

Paul raises his eyes. 'Ready, then?'

'Ready!'

'One, two, three – **GO!**'

Paul shouts the words and the two boys dive forward and swim. Fast and hard. Danny is quickly ahead.

'Bet you wish you weren't so heavy now, Benny!' Sarah calls.

Gruff has been lying next to John, eyes half closed. Suddenly he's up.

John glances at him; sees his nose twitch, then follows his gaze. Before he can stop him, Gruff scampers forwards.

'Hello, little dog. It's only me. D'you remember?'

John stands up. The other Topz twist round.

'Hey!' John grins. Gruff's tail beats the air happily. 'It's the boy from the hill.'

Josie smiles. 'Yeah. One of the leapfroggers. You were good.'

'Thanks,' says the boy.

There's a shout from the river. Danny has reached the far bank, but he doesn't climb out and wait for Benny. Instead he flips in the water and begins to race back.

'Wait!' gulps Benny. 'To the other side, you said.'

'Well, you're not here yet, are you?' puffs Danny. 'So I may as well see you back there.'

Danny dives past him going the other way.

'NOT FAIR!' shouts Benny. 'That's the last time I do any swim racing with you!'

The boy looks towards the river. 'Are they all right?'

'Oh, yeah,' says Dave. 'They're always like that.'

Sarah gets up and steps towards the newcomer. 'You never told us your name.'

'Isaac,' smiles the boy. 'My name's Isaac.'

'Well, Isaac, we were just dipping our feet,' Sarah says. 'Partly because it's really hot and partly because they're *really* dirty.'

John makes a face. 'Erm, I don't think Isaac wants to hear about your dirty feet, Sarah.'

'It's not just mine, is it?' answers Sarah. 'It's all this dust. We're all pretty filthy.'

John grunts. 'Sorry about my sister, Isaac. She's a bit like her cat. Obsessed with personal hygiene.'

'Personal what?' asks Isaac.

'Washing,' explains Paul.

'And what's wrong with that?' says Sarah.

'Yesss! We have a winner!' Danny yells from the bank. He heaves himself out of the water.

'No, we haven't!' splutters Benny. He's still only part way across. 'You can't have a winner if there's no race. And this isn't a race anymore because I've stopped racing!'

'Take no notice, Isaac,' says Dave. 'He's just a bit of a sore loser. So, what are you doing here?'

'Came for a swim,' Isaac replies. 'But maybe I could dip my feet with you for a bit first.' He glances at Sarah. 'They are quite dirty.'

'You see?' says Sarah. 'It's not just me.'

Benny stands on the bank, dripping. 'You're not the winner, Danny.'

'So what do *you* call it when you come first?' answers Danny.

'You didn't come first. This was not a race.'

'Started off as a race.'

'Well, that's not how it finished!'

'I think it is.'

'I THINK IT ISN'T!'

'Oh, stop it, you two!' says Josie. 'Can't you see we've got a visitor?'

Topz sit with Isaac in the shade on the bank. The river laps at their feet.

'Have you been listening to Him?' Isaac asks. 'Jesus. Have you been listening? I have. I've been following Him. I don't want to miss a thing He says. Mum says at least she knows where I am now. I was always wandering off, see? But now when she can't find me, she says she knows I'm safe. She knows I'm where the crowds are.'

'Jesus made two blind men see,' Dave says. 'It happened almost right in front of us. Benny and me.'

'And there's a fisherman in Capernaum,' adds Sarah. 'His mother-in-law was really ill and Jesus made her better.'

Isaac's eyes gleam. 'He's been going all over, this Jesus. From village to village. Town to town. Sometimes I'm worn out with all the walking. But Jesus – He doesn't seem to get worn out. He doesn't stop. He keeps travelling and teaching. Everywhere He goes, He teaches about God and God's kingdom. He tells people that He's come to lead them to God. That all they have to do is to turn away from the wrong things they do and believe that God sent Him – and then they can be with God in His kingdom forever.'

He pauses and kicks his feet in the water.

'Jesus loves everyone,' Isaac says. 'You can see it in His face. Deep down in His eyes. And I think it makes Him sad. He looks at the crowds of people and He sees how lost we are without God. We're all worried and scared and we don't know where we're going. Dad says we must look like sheep without a shepherd to Him, and it does – it makes Him sad. So that's why Jesus has come, isn't it? To show us God.

'And I heard Him say this thing to His friends,' he goes on. 'The special ones. The ones they call His disciples. I heard Jesus say, "The harvest is so big. But there aren't many harvesters to bring it in. Ask God, who owns the harvest, to send harvesters out, so that it can all be gathered in."'

He stops to glance round at his listeners. They sit still; quiet.

'I think I know what He means,' Isaac says. 'He means that there are people all over the place. All over the world. People who don't know who God is, but who really do need to know. They're the harvest. Only, Jesus can't get to everyone all by Himself. There are too many of them. So He needs helpers – harvesters – who will go to them and tell them about God, just like He does. Then they can be with God, too. That's what Jesus wants us to ask God for,' Isaac adds. 'Harvesters to bring in the harvest.'

The river trickles and flows and tugs coolly at the children's feet.

'That's what Jesus wants us to *be*, too,' John murmurs. 'Harvesters who bring in the harvest.'

CHAPTER 14
Under the Sky
(Matthew 10:26–30,40–42)

Sarah and Isaac stand on the very top of Jesus' hill. They gaze out at the views: the plains and the countryside, the lake and the clusters of houses.

'I love this hill,' Sarah says. 'This is where Jesus talked about how to pray, d'you remember? That's why I call it Jesus' hill. And down there's where we played leapfrog.'

Saucy burrows into the cradle of Isaac's arms. Isaac giggles.

'She likes you, Isaac,' says Sarah. 'Saucy doesn't snuggle with just anybody. Only the people she likes.'

'Sounds like our donkey,' Isaac smiles. 'Not that she snuggles with anyone. She doesn't do that. But she knows who she likes and who she doesn't. I think she'd like you. She wouldn't let you ride on her, but I think she'd like you.'

Sarah's eyes brighten. 'Could I meet her? I'd love to meet her. I'd probably be a bit scared to ride on her anyway. I tried riding a horse once and it was terrifying. It wouldn't do anything I wanted it to. I nearly fell off twice. Josie's really good at riding, though.'

'Well … we could go now,' Isaac says. 'Our donkey – she's called Beth. You could come and meet her now. If you want to.'

'I'd *love* to!'

So they walk, the two of them, with Saucy in Isaac's arms. Down the hill, along the dusty tracks, through the streets of Capernaum, to the very edge of the village.

'This is my house,' says Isaac. 'Beth's round the back.'

They slip through the front doorway into the kitchen. Freshly baked bread sits on a wooden table. The warm smell fills the air.

'My mum will have made that for later,' says Isaac. 'My dad's always starving when he gets home.'

A door in the back wall leads out to a small courtyard, where Beth is.

'I'll keep hold of Saucy,' says Isaac. 'You say hello.'

Beth looks half asleep under the hot sun. Her eyelids droop heavily. But as Sarah approaches with Isaac, she lifts her head.

Very slowly, Sarah holds out a hand. Beth eyes it a moment. Then, gently, she nuzzles it with her nose. Sarah turns and smiles at Isaac.

'I think you're right,' she says. 'I think Beth does like me.'

Isaac nods. 'I knew she would.'

Back out in the street, Saucy jumps to the ground.

'It's all right,' says Sarah. 'She can walk for a while.'

They turn a corner. Isaac stops.

On the ground under a tree, not far from them,

Jesus sits. His disciples are gathered around Him.
He talks to them.

'Don't be afraid of other people,' Jesus says. 'What I am teaching you about God – the things I am telling just to you – you must one day shout them from the rooftops! There will be people who won't like what you say. People who will want to hurt you for following me. But you mustn't be afraid of them. It's God you must think about.'

Jesus smiles. 'D'you know that for one penny you can buy two sparrows? Just one penny. But not even one sparrow dies without God agreeing to it. As for you, God has counted every single hair on your heads! That's how well He knows you! That's how much He loves you. So don't be frightened. You are more valuable than many, many sparrows to Him.'

Sarah steps closer. She sees the light dance in Jesus' eyes.

'If anyone you meet welcomes you,' Jesus goes on, 'then they welcome me, too. And if anyone welcomes me, then they welcome God, who sent me here.'

He pauses and looks around at His special friends, His disciples. Again He smiles. 'Remember that you are God's messengers. If someone greets you happily because of that – because you are God's messengers – that person will share in the great things God plans for you. The chance to live with God forever. If someone gives just a drink of cold water to someone else because they are a follower of mine, then God will bless them.'

Sarah notices Saucy padding further up the street. She nudges Isaac and nods her head towards her cat. She whispers, 'Let's go.'

They wander on together. They don't speak.

Sarah snatches a glance at Isaac. He seems quiet now. Preoccupied.

At last, 'Are you all right?' she asks.

'Yes,' Isaac answers. 'No … I don't know.'

They walk on in silence away from the village. Saucy scampers and prowls. With her paws, she bats at the air, at things only she can see.

Sarah tries again. 'I could help, maybe?'

'I'M JUST NOT BRAVE!' Isaac blurts out. 'Jesus wants friends who are brave. You heard Him. He wants friends who are brave enough to tell other people about Him. To tell other people that they belong to Him. That's what He said, Sarah … And I'm not brave.'

Sarah stops walking. She sits down.

'What are you doing?' asks Isaac.

'I'm hot so I'm sitting,' says Sarah. 'You can sit with me, if you like.'

Isaac stares at her a moment, crouches beside her and scribbles moodily in the dust with his finger.

'I'm not brave either, Isaac,' Sarah says. 'None of Topz are. Not *really* brave.'

'But you are. You must be. You're Jesus' friends.'

'Yes, we're Jesus' friends, but that doesn't make us brave. It doesn't mean we find it easy to tell people about Him. Especially people we might not like that much, or people who just don't want to know. But d'you know what helps?'

Isaac stares at her then shakes his head.

'Talking to God,' says Sarah. 'God can help me to be brave. When I ask for His help, God gives it to me.

He wants us to tell people about Him. He wants them to know. So He will make us brave enough. He'll make *you* brave enough, Isaac.'

Isaac drops his gaze. He ruffles the flat of his hand through his scribbles in the dust, rubbing them away.

'Will you pray for me, Sarah?' His voice is nervous. Hesitant.

Sarah smiles. 'Of course I will, Isaac.'

They close their eyes. They sit still out under the sky, and Sarah prays.

Father God, here am I and here is Isaac.

You know him so well. You have counted each hair on his head. You know everything about him. You know what makes him happy and what makes him sad.

And You know what makes him afraid.

Help Isaac to learn to trust You, Father God.

To remember that You promise to be with him when things are good and when things are bad.

That You will help him when he needs Your help.

And that You never break Your promises.

Isaac wants to be Your friend, Father God, and to shout it from the rooftops. So do I. We want to be brave.

So here am I, Father God, and here is Isaac. Amen.

CHAPTER 15
Rest
(Matthew 11:28–30)

They wake. Slowly, one by one.

Topz slept outside all night. The dark sky was full of stars. Tiny pinpoints of twinkling, flickering light. They laid on their backs on rugs and gazed up at them, until their eyelids grew heavy and they drifted off to sleep.

The sky is bright now and pale, cool blue. It's too early for the sun to have scorched it to its deeper colour.

John sits and stretches. He picks up a stick; pokes at the ashes from last night's campfire. They glow red-orange underneath.

'Still hot,' he says.

Benny stands. He yawns and rakes his hair back with his fingers. 'Hot enough to cook on?'

'Probably,' nods John. 'We could stoke it up.'

'Only one problem,' says Josie. 'We've got nothing left to cook.'

Benny looks horrified. 'What, nothing at all? But I'm starving.'

'You're always starving,' says Sarah.

'It's fine,' adds Danny. 'We can just walk back to Capernaum.'

'*Walk* back to Capernaum?' Benny's jaw drops. 'Before breakfast? Are you mad?'

'Put it this way, Benny.' Dave gets to his feet and starts to roll up his rug. 'There's not a lot of choice.'

Benny sighs and sinks down to sit near the embers of the fire. He grunts, 'Well, at least give me a chance to wake up properly first.'

Sarah stands, leaving Saucy still curled and sleeping on her rug. 'I'm going for a wash in the river.'

'Now there's a surprise,' John mutters.

'I'll come with you,' smiles Josie.

Instantly, Gruff is on his feet, too. He trots away after them.

'Huh!' John watches him go. 'Thanks a lot, Gruff. Nice to know who your friends are!'

Sarah and Josie lie on their stomachs on the riverbank. They cup their hands, scoop up water and splash their faces. The droplets fall through their fingers and glint and sparkle in the morning light. They hang their arms and hands down so that the river washes against them. They scramble up, sit and dangle their legs over the bank, kicking their feet in the cool of the shallows.

Gruff leaps into the water. He swims a little, turns and scrabbles out. He shakes himself dry and has a snuffle among the tree roots that twist and lace their way along the river's edge. Back he jumps into the water again.

Sarah and Josie watch him play.

'Why does Jesus have enemies?' Sarah asks.

Josie turns her head to look at her.

'When I was with Isaac yesterday,' Sarah says, 'we heard Jesus talking to the disciples. He said that there are people who won't like us if we try to tell them about Him. Why, Josie? Jesus does so much good. People love Him. Just look at the crowds that follow Him almost everywhere He goes. Why are there others who think His goodness is bad?'

Josie swirls her feet in the river. She watches the trails they make through the water; feels its softness against her ankles.

'There's a group that seems to want to make trouble for Jesus,' she answers. 'The Pharisees. That's what I've heard. The Pharisees think that they're right about the way to serve God, and that Jesus is wrong. They have so many different laws saying what they *should* do and what they *shouldn't* do. And what Jesus teaches about loving and forgiving each other just doesn't fit in with them.' Josie shrugs. 'That's why the Pharisees don't want people to follow Jesus. He upsets them because He tells people not to go along with their rules. He tells people to look at God instead. To look at God and follow *His* rules. And the Pharisees don't like it. They don't want to believe that Jesus is the Son of God.'

'But He is,' says Sarah. 'Look at everything He's doing. How can they not see that He *is* God's Son?'

Topz traipse back to Capernaum. Benny and Danny go in search of breakfast.

'Meet you back here,' says Benny.

But the others don't wait. They notice people

bustling past at the end of the street. They want to find out what's going on. They know they'll see Jesus.

He's teaching already. Listeners cluster round. Others further back crane their necks to see; to hear. Young and old; parents and grandparents and children.

Jesus spreads His arms wide. 'Come to me,' He says. 'Come to me right now – all of you who are tired. All of you who are full of worries and stresses and strains. Just come to me! I will give you rest. I will give you peace.

'I am a gentle Man,' Jesus says. 'I am a humble Man. I won't ask you to do anything that is too hard for you. I don't want to weigh you down with a heavy load. You will find rest if you will only come to me.'

Sarah feels tears prick at the back of her eyes.

She looks into the faces that stare out from the crowd. Some seem unsure. Others confused. Some beam with happiness.

'Look at them,' Sarah murmurs. 'Just look at them. They have someone to turn to now. Someone whose promises they can trust. Someone who wants to help them to live the best lives they can possibly live. Jesus can do all that – because Jesus can show them God!'

More and more people gather and jostle and fill the street.

'Seriously, just look at them all!' Sarah says. 'They're all so desperate to hear what He has got to say.'

She pushes back her hair; chews at her lip. 'So how can there be people who hate Him? Why would anyone hate the Man who's come to bring so much good news?'

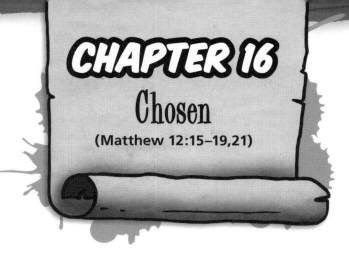

CHAPTER 16

Chosen

(Matthew 12:15–19,21)

Jesus keeps moving. He roams from place to place.
He works for God.

Topz never know where He will go next. Often they
follow Him; they see Him. Sometimes they hear news of
what He's done, things He's said; people He's healed.

And the crowds continue to follow Him, too. More and
more as word spreads about Him.

Every day He teaches them. Every day, sick people come
to Him or are brought to Him and He makes them well.

And with each miracle, His instructions are the same:
'Keep this to yourselves. Don't tell anyone about me.'

Paul stands on the edge of a large group with Dave.
They watch Jesus. They listen to His teaching.

'If you knew you were special,' Paul whispers, 'if you
knew you could do amazing things that no one else in
the whole world could do, would you want people to
keep quiet about it? Wouldn't you want everyone to be
talking about you?'

'Don't know.' Dave shrugs. 'I'm not really that
amazing so it's not something I think about.'

'Yeah, but if you *were*,' Paul says. 'What if you were – I dunno – the world's greatest bicycle repair person? I mean, what if you could put bikes back together in ways that other people had never even thought of? Ever! What if you'd *built* the fastest racing bike there has ever been? I mean, wouldn't you want to boast about it? Just a little bit? I know *I* would.'

Dave doesn't reply.

'But wouldn't you, Dave? Seriously, wouldn't you?'

Still no response.

Paul peers into his friend's face. 'Uh, hello? Is anyone in there?'

'I've read something ...' Dave says. He frowns, trying to remember. 'Something in the Bible about Jesus ... It's something God says about Him. Before Jesus was even born, God says what He'll be like. Jesus won't be boastful and loud, He'll be quiet. He won't make a huge big deal out of the incredible stuff He does because He's not doing it for Himself. He's doing it for God. And without God, He wouldn't be able to do it at all ... What was it I read? ... What *was* it? ... Oh, yeah. Now I remember ...'

'Here is my servant, whom I have chosen, the one I love, and with whom I am pleased. I will send my Spirit upon him ... He will not argue or shout, or make loud speeches in the streets ... and on him all peoples will put their hope.' (Matthew 12:18–19,21)

CHAPTER 17
What Heaven's Like
(Matthew 13:31–33,44–46)

Gruff is restless.

'I can't walk anymore, Gruff,' says John. 'It's too hot.'

'I don't think Gruff's too hot,' grins Benny.

'Gruff's never too hot,' moans John.

Let's go down to the lake,' suggests Josie. 'It might be cooler there.'

Sarah bends down to pick up Saucy.

Paul throws her a sideways look. 'Make sure you keep hold of her when we get there. And don't let her anywhere near the fishing boats. You know what happened last time. I'm not going sailing again. Not for anything.'

Sarah laughs and gives Saucy a hug. 'You hear that, Saucy?' she says, close to her cat's ear. 'Keep out of the fishing boats. Paul's sea legs are rubbish.'

'It's not just my legs,' grunts Paul. 'As far as boats go, it's all of me.'

As the village peters out and Topz reach the edge of the beach, a breeze wafts towards them. The air is warm, but the movement still cools them a little.

'Looks like everyone's had the same idea,' says Danny.

The lakeside is packed. There's no room for Gruff to run.

'I'll give you three guesses why,' says Josie. She stands on tiptoe and stretches to see over the heads of the crowds. She's not tall enough so instead she tries to peer in between the people crammed together in a dense huddle.

It's no good. Jesus is there. He must be. But none of Topz can see Him.

'OVER HERE!'

A boy further up the beach at the edge of the crowd shouts and waves his arms.

Sarah points. 'It's Isaac. I can see Isaac.'

He stands on his own on a rock that juts out of the ground above shingle. The Gang make their way towards him.

'Where is He?' asks Josie. 'Where's Jesus?'

Isaac nods towards the lake. From his perch on the rock, he can see it clearly. And he can see Jesus, who sits in a boat on the water and speaks to the listeners on the shore.

'Jesus had to go out on the lake,' Isaac says. 'He was on the beach but so many people came. So He got into the boat and pushed out from the lakeside. Now He can see us better. And more people can see Him and hear Him, too. I've been listening,' Isaac smiles. 'Jesus has been telling stories. He's been teaching with stories. If He uses stories, He says – stories about everyday things that we know about and understand – then that will help us to understand *Him*.'

Isaac budges up; makes room for the Gang on his rock.

'I hope I understand,' he says. 'I want to.'

'So do we,' says Danny. 'We'll try to understand together.'

'Do you know what the kingdom of heaven is like?' asks Jesus. 'Let me tell you. One day, a man takes a mustard seed. He goes out into his field and he plants it there in the earth.

'It is the tiniest of seeds, but what happens? It grows into an enormous plant! Its branches spread out. It becomes a tree! And what do you think happens next?' Jesus smiles. 'The birds see the tree and fly down to make their nests among the branches.'

'Where is the kingdom of heaven?' Isaac asks.

'It's where God lives,' answers Sarah. 'Where He's in charge. And one day we'll live there with Him, too. But until then, God wants us to make His kingdom here on earth – by living with Him as our best Friend. Living the way He wants us to.'

'And do you know what else the kingdom of heaven is like?' asks Jesus. 'It's like this. A woman gets ready to do some baking. She measures out forty litres of flour. Then she mixes a small amount of yeast into it. That yeast is enough to make the whole batch of dough rise.'

Jesus adds, 'And the kingdom of heaven is priceless, too! Listen. A man is digging in a field, when what does he find? Treasure! Hidden in the ground. The man is so excited that he doesn't just grab the treasure and take it with him. No! He covers it up again. Then he goes home, sells everything he has, and with the money, he buys the whole field! That's how precious the treasure is to him. That's how precious God wants the kingdom of heaven to be to us.

'And what about a man who goes out looking for beautiful pearls? He finds one that is more than beautiful. It's spectacular! So he goes and sells everything he has, too – so that he can buy that pearl. God wants the kingdom of heaven to be as precious to us as that.'

Isaac listens, eyes wide.

'Come and camp with us tonight,' whispers Sarah. 'We can tell stories round the campfire.'

Later, as darkness falls, Topz heap up dry sticks inside a circle of stones on the ground, and sit on rugs around dancing, crackling flames. They munch on bread baked by Isaac's mum. They talk about Jesus' stories.

'God wants us to make living His way the most important thing we do,' says Dave. 'He hopes we'll want to be a part of His kingdom more than anything else.'

'As precious as a pearl and as priceless as treasure in a field,' nods Isaac. 'That's how He wants us to feel about our friendship with Him. I get that. But there were other stories. A mustard seed and yeast. What do those stories mean?'

Josie throws another piece of wood on the fire. Benny pushes a piece of bread onto the end of stick, holds it out to the flames and watches it as it toasts.

'God's kingdom is like a mustard seed,' says Josie, 'because it started in a tiny way, and now it's growing. Think about it, Isaac,' she smiles. 'Jesus only had a few followers to start with. Topz and me – we saw Him call them. Down by the lake. Simon Peter, Andrew, James and John. He called them and they followed Him.

'But then He started to call others, too. And He began to teach people. And heal people. And suddenly those few followers turned into lots more.'

Isaac's eyes shine, reflecting the glow from the campfire flames as they leap and play. 'There'll be more and more, too, won't there? As more people get to hear.'

Josie nods. 'So the kingdom of God grows from tiny beginnings. That's why it's like a mustard seed.'

'So it's like yeast,' says Isaac, 'because yeast makes the flour it touches swell and grow, too. More and more people will hear about Jesus, and more and more people will be affected by His teaching and His miracles. So God's kingdom will grow like yeasty dough.' He laughs. 'Like my mum's bread!'

'It's good bread,' says Benny. He slips the piece he's been toasting off the end of the stick and crunches into it. 'And it makes stonkingly good toast.'

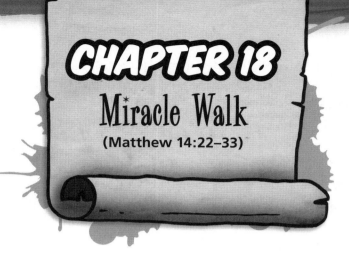

CHAPTER 18
Miracle Walk
(Matthew 14:22–33)

John can't sleep. He's restless. Can't get comfortable.
Every so often, he drops off for a few moments.
Suddenly, he's wide awake again. Each time he fidgets
or turns over on his rug, Gruff opens an eye and nudges
John with his nose.

'No, Gruff,' mutters John. 'How do you always
know when I'm awake? This isn't fuss time, it's rest
time. Time for you to sleep. Time for *me* to sleep.
Except I can't.'

Jesus' stories run around John's head. God's kingdom
growing like a mustard seed; its pricelessness.
The preciousness of being a part of it.

He sits up. The other Topz and Isaac are fast asleep.
Saucy snuggles into Sarah. It's only he and Gruff who
are awake.

He wonders what time it is. Very late or very early?
Everywhere is still. Silent. The sky overhead is a deep
dark blue. It glitters with stars and the moon is up.
Full and silver.

'Where's Jesus now?' John wonders.

When He had finished teaching the evening before, and in dribs and drabs the people had begun to drift back to their homes, Jesus hadn't stayed with His disciples.

'Take the boat,' He had said to them. 'Go on ahead of me to the other side of the lake.'

So, as the lakeside emptied of onlookers and night drew in, Jesus' disciples had climbed into the boat and set sail.

Now Jesus could spend some time by Himself.

For a short while, no crowds. No questions, no demands.

And He had made His way to a hillside where He could be alone.

But however tired He was, He didn't rest there. He didn't sleep.

Jesus wanted to be alone so that He could talk to God. He needed God to refresh Him.

John gets up. Pointless to lie there any longer. Gruff gets to his feet, too. Expectant, tail wagging.

'No, Gruff,' John whispers. 'Stay here. I'm just going for a wander. Stay.'

He creeps quietly away from the camp and his sleeping friends. Gruff ignores the command; trots cheerfully at his heels. Two night-walkers together.

They follow the track that leads back towards the lake. John keeps to a route he knows. He doesn't want to get lost in the dark. Gruff stays close.

Ahead of them, a hill rises up. Steep and curved and without trees. A shadowy shape under the moon.

'Shall we climb the hill, Gruff?' says John. 'Let's get nearer the moon and go up the hill.'

As they reach its foot, a breeze begins to blow in from the direction of the lake. They start their walk up the slope. It isn't very steep but the higher they climb, the stronger the wind blows. It snatches at John's breath. He pauses. Gruff scampers on ahead.

At the top, John sees the lake spread out below them. The water comes alive as the breeze grows wilder. It heaves and churns and white-tipped waves build and run and break. The stars overhead seem a little less bright, and a golden glow begins to lighten the strip of sky stretched along the horizon.

'I think dawn's on its way, Gruff,' murmurs John. 'We've been awake pretty much all night.'

His face is buffeted by the wind but it's cool and fresh and he doesn't care.

As the daylight slowly grows, that's when he sees the boat. A boat a long way out on the lake. He watches as it's thrown up and down and rocked from side to side by the wind and the waves.

Someone else watches the boat, too.

A figure below on the beach.

John's eyes widen. 'It's Jesus! Gruff, it's Jesus.'

As the sun starts to spread fingers of gleaming light above the line of the horizon, Jesus steps into the water.

John frowns. 'What's He doing? What's He doing, Gruff? He mustn't go in the water, it's too rough. Way too rough. He might get swept out.'

Jesus begins to walk through the bubbling shallows out towards the boat.

John doesn't hesitate. He runs. 'Come on, Gruff! Come on!'

They hurtle together. Across the hilltop and down the far flank that curves towards the lakeside. They scamper and slide and scrabble all the way down to the scrubby ground that leads onto the beach. They tear across shingle, then sand; stopping only when they reach the water's edge.

They stop abruptly.

As the light of dawn starts to creep up and over the arc of the sky, John can see Jesus. He is illuminated out on the heaving lake.

And John sees for the first time that Jesus isn't walking through the waves; He doesn't have to drag His legs through the swirling currents and struggle to stay upright as the waves swell and slap against Him. Jesus is somehow above them.

Jesus is walking *on* the water.

John doesn't breathe. He can't. He can only brace himself against the strengthening wind and stare in complete astonishment.

He hears a voice. Several voices shouting. Carried towards him on the wild air.

'It's a ghost! It's a ghost! Look, there! A ghost!'

And there are screams of terror.

But then John hears Jesus. Jesus' voice is strong and clear. It cuts through the stormy air.

'Be brave!' He cries. 'It's me! Just me. There's nothing to be scared of.'

John takes a couple of steps forwards. He squints

towards the boat; sees one of the sailors stand up, haul himself to the side to get a closer look at the figure on the water.

'IS IT REALLY YOU, LORD?' shouts the sailor.

It's Peter. That's Peter's voice.

'If it really is You, order me to get out of the boat and walk on the water over to You.'

Jesus' voice rings out again. Deep and purposeful. 'Come on then, Peter!'

John watches Peter pull himself up and over the side of the boat; sees him hold on for one second more – then step onto the lake. One foot, then the other. One foot, then the other. And Peter walks on the water, too. Straight towards Jesus.

'Can you see that, Gruff?' gasps John. 'Can you see it?' He jumps up and down, whoops and punches the air in excitement.

But then he looks at Peter again. And he freezes. 'No ...'

Peter is in trouble. He's taken his eyes off Jesus. He looks around. He feels the strength of the wind. He sees the height of the waves.

And in terror, he begins to sink down into them.

They arch and roar and threaten to close over his head.

'Jesus, save me! Save me, Lord, please save me!'

Jesus is immediately next to him. He reaches out and grabs hold of the petrified, sinking man. He hauls him up.

'Oh, Peter,' He says. 'You don't have much faith in me, do you? Why did you doubt me?'

Jesus helps Peter back towards the boat; helps him climb up into it, then clambers in after him.

Almost at once, the wind dies away. The waves on the lake settle down. The boat on the water barely bobs.

Then John hears them, the fishermen sailors. He hears them exclaim, 'Jesus! You truly are the Son of God!'

And on the beach, in the very early morning, John sinks to his knees.

'Yes, Jesus,' he murmurs. 'You truly are God's Son.'

CHAPTER 19
Miracle Faith

'JOHN!'

Sarah's yell is heard across the beach: 'John, are you all right?'

Fishermen turn to look.

She starts to run. Isaac and the other Topz run with her. Gruff lifts his head at the sound of Sarah's voice. He leaves John's side and pelts towards her.

'Is he all right, Gruff?' asks Sarah. She slows as the little dog leaps around her in excitement. 'Come on, show me!'

John sits cross-legged down by the water. He hasn't moved since he watched Jesus and Peter climb safely back into the boat.

There's no sign of the boat now. As the sun climbed in the sky, Jesus and His disciples had landed on the other side of the lake at Gennesaret.

John had stayed where he was. Exactly at the spot where he'd seen the water-walking miracle. He didn't want to move; didn't want to risk losing the sense of God's awesomeness that had filled him as he watched.

'John!' Sarah reaches him.

He turns his head and smiles up at her. At the others, too, as they gather round him.

'Why did you leave?' Sarah puffs. 'I woke up and you were gone. What's wrong? Why did you go? We thought something had happened to you.'

John shrugs. 'I couldn't sleep. I tried. I lay there for ages and ages, but I couldn't sleep. So I thought I'd go for a walk.'

'In the middle of the night?' Sarah frowns. 'On your own – without us?'

'I wasn't on my own,' John answers. 'Gruff came with me and I didn't mean to go far. I certainly didn't mean to be long. Only, suddenly it was getting light. We'd been awake almost all night, him and me and ...' He trails off.

'What, John? What?'

John swallows, looking intently into his sister's face. Into the faces of his friends.

'If I tell you something, you have to believe me,' he says. 'I didn't imagine it and I'm not making it up. I saw it, Sarah. And I have to tell you what I saw.'

'Of course we'll believe you,' Sarah answers. 'Just tell us.'

They sit all together at the lakeside and John describes to them how Jesus and Peter had walked out on the wind-whipped lake; how Peter had only begun to fall into the waves when he took his eyes off Jesus.

'But Jesus saved him,' says John. 'He grabbed hold of him and He helped him back on the boat.

Do you see, though?' John asks. He glances at Isaac then looks around at Sarah; at each of his friends. 'Do you see what faith can do? Jesus called Peter out onto the water, and Peter had the faith to obey Him. He only got in trouble when he *stopped trusting* Jesus.' John shakes his head. 'And he had no reason to stop trusting Him. Jesus can walk on water! He's the Son of God, and the Son of God is never going to let us down. Why would He?'

'It's hard to have faith like that all the time, John.' Danny picks at shells and stones along the water line. 'Faith that Jesus will help you with the everyday stuff, let alone the tricky, impossible stuff. Faith that doesn't get rocked.'

John nods. 'I know. So we've got to ask God to *help* us have faith like that. Faith for the little tiny things. And faith to believe in the unbelievable, too.'

He looks out across the lake and pictures Jesus where he'd seen Him a few hours earlier, walking on the water.

'That's what I've been doing,' he says. 'Here on the beach, that's what I've been asking God for – the sort of trust that doesn't just come and go. That doesn't depend on me being in a good mood or on things turning out my way. That doesn't rely on whether *I* think something's possible! I want to trust God however I feel and whatever I think. Because faith like that – it works miracles.'

Isaac's head droops. 'I wish I'd seen Him,' he mumbles. He sounds sad; disappointed. 'I wish you'd woken me up and I'd come with you, and then I'd have seen Jesus walk on water. I wish I could have seen it, too.'

'It doesn't matter.' John shakes his head again. 'Don't you see that, Isaac? It doesn't matter that you didn't see. Just choose to believe that Jesus is God's Son and ask God to help you to trust Him. And that's what He'll do. He'll help you to have faith. He will, Isaac. Because that's what He wants for everyone in the whole world. He just wants us to have faith.'

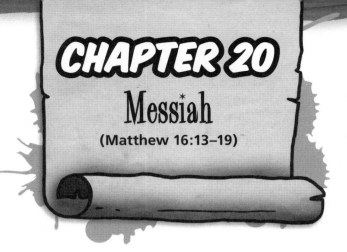

CHAPTER 20

Messiah

(Matthew 16:13–19)

The miracles go on.

Jesus heals sick people across the lake in Gennesaret.

He travels to a place near the cities of Tyre and Sidon. He works hard for His Father God.

And when He moves on, along the shores of Lake Galilee, still people flock to Him. They bring with them the ones who are sick, the ones who can't walk, who can't see; who can't speak.

And those people leave healed – completely well – running and skipping and gazing in wonder and praising God with their mouths and their tongues, in cries and shouts and yells.

Topz follow Jesus, too. Wherever He goes.

All they want is to be close to Him, to hear more of His teaching; to see what He will do next.

They follow Jesus to a place some way from Capernaum. A place near a town called Caesarea Philippi. They sit down to rest, eat some bread and drink some water.

Benny finds a stick and they play a game in the dust.

'I'll start to draw something,' says Benny, 'and you've got to guess what it is.'

He scratches a straight line horizontally in the rough, dry ground. 'Well?'

'It's a straight line, Benny,' says Dave. 'It could be anything.'

'Exactly,' says Benny. 'So have a guess.'

Dave shrugs. 'I dunno ... A house ...'

NAAH! grins Benny. 'A house would be way too easy.'

He scratches another line – in the centre of the first line, shorter and sticking up.

Paul squints at it. 'A flower?' he suggests.

Benny makes a face. 'How does that look like a flower?'

'Well, it could be,' says Paul. 'In the ground. Just without the flower bit on yet.'

'Think again,' Benny says, and this time he draws a circle under one end of the long line.

Paul stares at it; blows his cheeks out. 'No idea.'

'Maybe ... a boat?' says Sarah.

'A boat?' answers Benny. 'Doesn't look anything like a boat.'

Sarah points to the circle. 'Well, that could be a window. You know, one of those porthole thingies.'

Benny shakes his head. He looks smug. 'It could be but it's not.'

This time he draws a very short line across the top of the sticking up line.

'A bicycle!' Josie chirps.

And Benny's face falls. 'How on earth could you

get bicycle from that?' He jabs the stick into his unfinished picture.

'Just genius, I guess,' smiles Josie. 'It is though, isn't it? It's a bicycle.'

'Tsh ...' sighs Benny. 'I thought it'd take you ages. All right, yes, it's a bicycle.'

'Ha!' says John. 'Good one, Benny. Go on then, finish it. Finish the drawing.'

Reluctantly Benny scratches the rest of the outline into the dust. The other wheel, the handlebars.

'Cool looking bike,' says Danny.

'I tell you what, I wish I *had* a bike,' grunts Benny. 'All this walking. It's wearing me out.'

They look up and see Jesus. He and His disciples are close to where Topz sit playing Benny's game.

They talk.

Jesus says, 'Tell me. What do people say about the Son of Man? Who do they think I am? Who do they *say* I am?'

Jesus' friends answer.

'I've heard some people say John the Baptist.'

'And there are some who say the prophet, Elijah.'

'Or the prophet, Jeremiah. Or one of the other prophets.'

They speak together, blurting out what they know – the gossip; the rumours they've heard.

Jesus gazes round at them. His eyes are serious. His expression intense.

'What about you?' He asks. 'What do *you* think? Who do you say I am?'

Simon Peter doesn't hesitate. He doesn't have to. He knows the answer.

'You are the Messiah,' he says. 'You are the Son of the living God.'

Jesus stares at Him. The seriousness in His eyes melts away. A smile spreads across His face.

'Well done, Simon Peter!' He grins. 'That is exactly who I am. No other human being can have told you this. This truth has come to you straight from God. Straight from my Father in heaven.'

Simon Peter returns Jesus' gaze; unsure what to think or what to say.

'Listen to me, Peter,' smiles Jesus. 'From now on, you will be like a rock – solid and firm. I will build my Church on this rock. My Church of people who believe who I am; who want to put God at the very centre of their lives. And the foundations of this Church will be so strong that not even death will be able to destroy it.

'Peter,' Jesus continues with excitement in His voice. 'Peter, I am going to give you the keys to the kingdom of heaven. Do you understand? What you don't allow here on earth will not be allowed in heaven. And what you *do* allow on earth will be allowed in heaven.'

Peter catches his breath. He looks open mouthed into Jesus' face. Is this real? What is he hearing? How can he believe that Jesus has singled him out like this?

Yet how can he not believe it? Jesus only ever tells the truth.

'What are the keys?' whispers Sarah. 'What has Jesus given to Peter? I don't understand.'

'They're not *actual* keys,' murmurs Dave. 'I think ...
I think Jesus has just made Peter a leader. In charge of
spreading the news about Him. Of telling people who
He is and who God is. In charge of helping them to
make friends with Him.'

Topz watch. For another moment the disciples stay
grouped around Jesus. The Gang wait for more. For Jesus
to explain more or for Peter to answer.

But there's nothing now. Jesus and His disciples walk on.
Dave gets to his feet and watches them go.

'Peter will be able to open the door to understanding
who God is. For everyone he chooses to speak to,' he
says. 'That's how the Church will really begin to grow
and grow. Through what Peter does and what Peter
says. Jesus has made him into a leader.'

Topz don't go back to their game. It doesn't seem
important now.

They scramble up, following at a distance behind
Jesus. Behind His troop of special friends.

'I wonder how it feels,' says Josie, 'to be one of Jesus'
disciples? It must be amazing.'

'But you *are* one of His disciples,' answers Dave. 'We all
are, aren't we? We follow Jesus and we want to learn from
Him. That's what disciples do.'

He smiles. 'We're all His friends, Josie. And it's up to
His friends to help Jesus' Church to grow.'

CHAPTER 21
He Will
(Matthew 16:21–27)

'Can you skip stones?' asks Danny.

Isaac stands with him at the lake edge.

'On the water?' says Isaac. 'Of course I can.'

He crouches down; pokes about in the scatter of pebbles at his feet. 'Got one.'

He picks up a flattish stone and, keeping low, angles himself towards the water. With a flick of his wrist, he lets it fly. It skims the surface of the lake, then skips six times before it disappears into the depths.

'Whoa!' cries Danny. 'You got *six*! That's impressive, Isaac. Even Benny's never got six! And four's my record.'

Isaac grins. 'Try now. Lake's calm. It's easier when it's calm.'

Danny scrabbles among the pebbles. He finds one about the same shape and size as Isaac's six scorer. He goes to throw it.

'Lower,' says Isaac. 'Get lower to the water.'

Danny twists his waist, bends his knees, flicks the stone. But the throw is awkward and the stone sinks on the second bounce.

'You're too tense,' says Isaac. 'You've just got to move with it.'

He finds another pebble. He dips his body, aims at the water, flicks his wrist smoothly and easily and they watch the stone fly, then skip across the surface. Again, six times.

Danny shakes his head. 'You're too good at this.'

Isaac shrugs; searches the water line for another stone.

'Everyone's talking about Jesus,' he says. 'In the village. It feels like no one's ever talked about anything else. Like Jesus has been here forever.'

He fires off another stone and sends it dancing out across the lake.

'Five, I think,' Danny says.

'One day I'll get ten,' answers Isaac. 'That's what I'm aiming for. Ten.'

The two boys gaze out at the water. There are fishing boats in the distance. They can just make out the fishermen working. Hauling in the nets.

'Do you think He'll stay around, Danny?' Isaac asks.

'JESUS?'

Danny glances at him. Just quickly.

'I hope He does,' Isaac says. 'I want Him to. I hope He does.'

In the sky overhead, white clouds glide above the lake. So slowly, they hardly move at all.

And across the stillness of the beach, voices drift towards them.

Isaac smiles. 'Jesus.'

Jesus sits on a rock further up the lakeside.

The same rock Isaac had stood on to listen to His teaching. This time there are no crowds on the shore to press in around Him. Jesus speaks just to His troop of disciples.

'I have to go to Jerusalem.'

The two boys can't help but overhear.

'I have to go there ... And I will be made to suffer there.'

A frown crosses Isaac's face. He looks at Danny; looks immediately back towards Jesus.

'The chief priests and the religious teachers,' Jesus sighs, 'they don't like me. They hate me. They hate what I say because it doesn't fit in with their rules, or how they think things should be. They don't believe that I'm God's Son. They will put me to death.'

Isaac draws in a breath. Sudden. Sharp. As if he's in pain.

'BUT, LISTEN!' Jesus says. **'WITHIN THREE DAYS, I WILL COME BACK TO LIFE.'**

Peter scowls. He shakes his head, not listening to these last few words. He beckons Jesus away from the group.

'No, Lord, never!' he snarls. 'Never! God forbid that anyone should ever hurt You. This must *never* happen to You!'

Jesus turns on him. His eyes look dark as He glares at the angry disciple.

'Get away from me!' Jesus' voice is quiet but strong. 'Do you hear me? Away! You are a block on my path. What you say doesn't come from God. It comes from your own selfishness. From your own selfish thoughts and wants.'

Peter stands. Confused. Almost frightened.

Jesus says to His disciples, 'People who want to come with me must forget that selfish part of themselves. They must follow me without looking back. Those who want to hang on to their selfish lives will never find God. But those who give them up – who give their lives to me and let God be in control – those people will find more life than they could ever imagine. Life with God forever!'

The group of disciples listen. There is sadness in their faces, but a look of wonder, a look of curiosity, too.

Jesus gazes out towards the lake; spreads His arms wide.

'What's the good of owning all of this – the whole world even – if it means giving up being with God? What's the point? There's no point at all!'

He pauses. He turns His face back to His disciples.

'One day I will come to the earth again. Through my Father God's power. And when I do, I will reward my friends according to what they have done and how they have lived their lives.'

Isaac watches for a moment more. Then, 'I'm going home,' he murmurs.

'I'll walk with you,' says Danny.

'No. I want to be on my own.'

'Then I'll just go with you a little way.'

They walk in silence. Isaac keeps his head down; kicks at stones and driftwood on the beach.

'He's coming back,' Danny says finally. 'Jesus says He's coming back.'

Isaac stops still. 'But why does He have to go?'

he blurts out. 'Why are there people who hate Him? **HE HELPS US. HE CHANGES LIVES.** He turns them upside down. He's changed *my* life, Danny!'

He pauses. His shoulders droop. Tears glisten in his eyes and spill down his face. He brushes them from his cheeks with his fists.

'So why are there people who want Him dead? I don't get it. Everything He does is good. Why do people want Him to die?'

Isaac looks into Danny's face; intently into his eyes, searching for reassurance.

'If God has a plan for everyone – and He does, a plan and a purpose,' Danny says slowly, 'then He knows what He's doing. We have to trust Him, Isaac. Trust that He knows what He's doing and that everything He does will be for the best.'

Isaac screws up his face. 'But how can this be for the best? How can Jesus *dying* be for the best?'

'Because He'll come back to life,' says Danny. 'You heard Him. He'll come back to life! And when He does, Isaac, that's how we'll get to be with God forever.'

Isaac still stares at him.

'All the wrong things we do,' Danny goes on, 'they spoil our friendship with God. They make it hard for Him to even look at us. But when Jesus dies, He'll take all those wrong things away. Then each time we tell God we're sorry – truly sorry – He'll forgive us. He'll make our friendship with Him brand new again.'

Isaac glances over His shoulder at the disciples on the shore; at Jesus.

'But what if it doesn't happen?' he asks. 'What if Jesus doesn't come back to life?'

Danny looks towards Jesus, too. 'He will, Isaac … He will.'

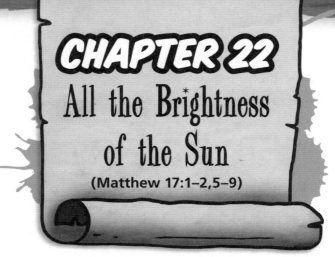

CHAPTER 22
All the Brightness of the Sun
(Matthew 17:1–2,5–9)

Topz run sprint races.

Back and forth.

Gruff bounds along after John, barking madly.

Saucy lies, eyes closed, stretched lazily in the sunshine.

'I won!' shrieks Benny.

'What, again?' frowns John.

'You always say that,' puffs Josie.

'That's because I always win,' Benny grins.

'No, you don't,' says Paul. 'I mean, you always beat me, but that's different. Nearly everyone always beats me. But I reckon that time it was Danny.'

'Thanks for pointing that out, Paul,' says Danny. 'I think it was me, too.'

'We need someone on the finish line,' suggests Dave. 'Someone to see who really does come in first.'

John sticks up his hand. 'I'll do it. I'm worn out running anyway.'

He flops down under the tree they're using as a finish post. 'I can start you off properly, too.'

Topz line up, ready to race again.

'Actually,' says Sarah, 'I'm with John. Can't be bothered to run anymore. I think I'm gonna go exploring with Saucy.'

'D'you want me to come with you?' asks Josie.

'No, I'm all right,' answers Sarah. 'I feel like being intrepid.'

Benny throws her a sideways glance. 'In-*what*-id?'

'Intrepid,' says Sarah. 'You know. Brave and daring. Like an explorer.'

'Oh,' nods Benny. 'Cool.'

Sarah bends down, lifts Saucy up and into her open shoulder bag. Saucy's head and front paws pop out of the top. She watches where they're going.

'Come on, cat,' Sarah says. 'Let's be intrepid together.'

In the distance, a mountain points ruggedly upwards towards the sky.

'We'll catch you up!' shouts Josie.

'Great!' Sarah calls back. 'We're heading *that* way!'

To Saucy, she whispers, 'Let's do it, Saucy. Let's go climb a mountain.'

Sarah walks and the mountain gets closer. With every step it looms wider and higher. And lonelier.

The slope is gentle to start with. Barely a climb at all. But the further Sarah goes, the more the mountainside steepens and the harder it is.

She pauses, out of breath; turns. Already the views across the plains are magnificent.

'Look at it, Saucy,' she murmurs. 'Look how beautiful it is here. Jesus has come to live somewhere amazing.'

She continues to climb. Up and up. Slower sometimes to recover, then more quickly. She stops now and again to catch her breath. To gaze at the land that lies beneath them; fans out around them.

At last she reaches a spot where the mountain slope begins to level out.

'PHEW, SAUCY!' she gasps. **'THAT WAS HARD WORK!'**

She crosses the flatter part and sinks down to rest, with her back against an outcrop of rock. Her blood throbs at her temples.

'It's all right for you,' she puffs. 'All the great views – none of the effort!'

Saucy wriggles. She pulls herself out of Sarah's bag and circles in her lap, then snuggles down. In the cosiest spot. In the most comfortable position.

Sarah leans her head back against the rock; closes her eyes.

Seconds later, she snaps them open.

There's movement behind her.

She's not alone.

Still sitting, Sarah shuffles closer to the outside edge of her rock support and peers around it.

On the same level spot of mountainside, she sees Jesus. He's with Peter, James and John. She didn't notice them as she climbed. They must have made their way up the other side.

But why are they here?

Of all places, why would Jesus bring His friends to somewhere so remote?

It's a tough climb. A very tough climb. He must want to make completely sure that they're not followed.

And all of a sudden, Sarah sees why.

As Jesus' friends look at Him – as *she* stares at Him – it's as if He becomes bathed in light. But the light touches only Him.

Jesus' face shines with all the brightness of the sun. His clothes gleam a dazzling white.

Sarah screws up her eyes, but the glare is too great. She has to look away a moment; has to force herself to look back.

That's when she sees the cloud. An extraordinary, shining cloud. It seems to hover over Jesus and His friends. Peter, James and John are transfixed by it.

Sarah shifts a little further along behind her rock to get a better look.

She hears a voice. She freezes.

The voice speaks from out of the cloud. It's a voice she's heard before. Days and days and days ago when Jesus was baptised in the River Jordan.

And she thinks her heart will stop.

'This is my Son. My very own Son, and I am so pleased with Him. You must always listen to Him.'

The three disciples must think their hearts might stop, too.

At the sound of the voice, they turn white. They are scared half to death. They throw themselves on the ground. Face down, they lie there and tremble.

Until Jesus goes to them; touches them with a reassuring hand.

'It's all right,' He says. 'You can get up. There's nothing to be afraid of. See?'

Slowly, reluctantly, they lift their heads. Still frightened, they glance about them.

The cloud has gone. In front of them, there is just Jesus.

They scramble to their feet. They seem stunned; in a daze.

'We must go back now,' says Jesus. 'And you must do this for me: you must not tell anyone – no one at all – what you have seen and heard here. Do you understand? You're not to speak of it. Not until after God has brought me back to life.'

Sarah stays hidden. She watches as Jesus leads His friends away from the loneliness of the mountain; loses sight of them when they disappear down the steep slopes that will take them to the ground. Back to the clamouring crowds of people who are so desperate to know God.

Absent-mindedly, Sarah strokes Saucy's ears. Now and again, the little cat flicks them in protest. She wants to sleep. To enjoy the warmth of the sun on her fur. The comfort and safety of Sarah's lap. She doesn't want to be disturbed.

Sarah doesn't want to be disturbed either.

She feels the way John felt on the lake shore after he'd watched Jesus walk on water.

She's seen Jesus burn with light.

She's witnessed God's power; she's heard His voice.

And she never wants to let the feeling go.

The air is still. Cool now as the sun slips down.

Another day drifts into evening. Another night to come.

Sarah walks carefully, Saucy tucked back into her bag. She braces her knees against the steepest slopes of the mountainside. And the mountain's shadow grows long, soft and blue-grey and stretched out across the plains.

'There she is!' Josie waves madly. 'Sarah!'

'Talk about pulling a disappearing act!' shouts Benny. 'We've been looking everywhere.'

'Where have you been?' calls John. 'Not up the mountain? You didn't climb up the mountain?'

Sarah smiles. 'Yes!' she whispers to herself. 'Yes, I climbed up the mountain! And what I saw there will stay with me for all of my life.'

She pulls Saucy from the shoulder bag and hugs her close. Their single shadow lengthens and ripples and trails along after them.

'FOR ALL OF MY LIFE ...'

Colourful daily Bible reading notes just for you

In each issue the Topz Gang teach you biblical truths through word games, puzzles, riddles, cartoons, competitions, simple prayers and daily Bible readings.

Available as an annual subscription or as single issues.

For current prices or to purchase go to **www.cwr.org.uk/store** call 01252 784700 or visit a Christian bookshop.